THE
WU
WAY

A Path to Natural Healing

MARK DANA MINCOLLA, Ph.D.

Pennyroyal Press

Copyright © 1992 by Mark Dana Mincolla
Illustrations copyright © 1992 by Barbara Alger

All rights reserved under International and Pan-American Copyright
Conventions. Published in the United States by Pennyroyal Press, Inc.

The theories presented here are based on the author's in-depth work and
research. They should not be put into practice without prior consultation
with a licensed medical professional.

Library of Congress Catalog Card Number: TXU 510512

ISBN: 0-9632811-0-0

Cover Design by Barbara Alger
Illustrations by Barbara Alger
Text Design and Layout by Susan Curtis
Text Typing by Anne Montague
Photography by Robert Coletti

Manufactured in the United States of America

First Edition: December 1992

To my dear Pop
who endeavored as my partner with this book
but now serves as my heartfelt inspiration
since he unexpectedly left this world
a few short months before its completion.
If only this book could give the world a mere glimmer
of the light and love that he gave to me.

To Nick and Lex
It is with every fiber of my being
that I hope to make some small contribution
of love and healing to an ailing world,
so that theirs may be a brighter future.

. . . "Thus then to man the voice of Nature spake
Go, from the creatures thy instructions take:
Learn from the birds the foods the thickets yield;
Learn from the beasts the physic of the field;
The arts of building from the bee receive;
Learn of the mole to plow, the worm to weave;
Learn of the little nautilus to sail,
Spread the thin air, and catch the driving gale . . .
How those in common all their wealth bestow,
And anarchy without confusion know;
Mark what unvaried laws preserve each state,
Laws wise as Nature, and fixed as Fate . . ."

Essays on Man Epistle III, 1726
Selected works of Alexander Pope
The Modern Library, NY, 1948

Acknowledgements

First, I must thank Anne. If not for her tireless giving every step of the way, there would be no *Wu Way*. Thanks also to Barbara and Susan for sharing their remarkable talents and skills.

Thanks to my clients for teaching me to teach.

To my wife Cecilia and my two sons, Nick and Lex who put up with me over the past three-and-one-half years as this book became a reality. I am indebted to them.

Thanks to my dad for being my earthly partner at the beginning of this project, and my guardian angel the rest of the way.

And, love and adoration to a God who in His wisdom brought us all together.

M.D.M.

Table of Contents

Preface

Throughout the past ten years of my private wholistic counseling practice, the over twenty thousand consultations I have rendered have given me the opportunity to observe and facilitate respectively the loss and the reattainment of the subtle, precious, mysterious "force of life."

With each individual consultation I became increasingly aware that each of us is fully equipped with the potential for profound healing. Also, it became clear that many who came to me for my observations were, in fact, blind to their own healing force, and that I merely passed back to them only that which they chose not to see.

I believe that we have arrived at a time where we no longer understand or appreciate this innate natural healing potential. We have lost touch with such subtle forces of nature, including the basic nature of our own body, mind, and spirit, and their relationship to the Earth/Universe. The price has been all too costly.

We are all born of nature, organic and natural just as the trees, the wind, and the water. This organic nature naturally emanates through us, just as it is within us. Yet we have become divorced and desensitized from this natural presence, choosing instead to become more synthetic, artificial, technological, and scientific. The result of this disharmony is what I call "de-evolutionary sickness," the "mother of disease." When we are harmonious with nature, wellness prevails; when we rebel from this instinct, disease prevails.

In spite of our rebellious ego, we are still bound by nature; we are still children of nature, and the single most important step on the path to genuine healing remains the conceptual acceptance of this fact. True healing begins with the awareness of, and the surrender to the dictates of natural life or the understanding of, and compliance with subtle natural law. Before one can eat, think, or heal naturally, one must first elevate his consciousness so as to allow the innate subtle force of nature to pass through them, undisturbed as it was intended, without obstruction, without denial.

Over the years, there have been endless attempts to define and to interpret the term wholistic (holistic). The word wholistic is most generally used in healing circles as a generic term for treating the whole person, body, mind, and spirit, rather than the symptoms or disease. It has been, however, bastardized, bent and shaped as a catch word to grace everything from astrology to mega-vitamin therapy. It was again through my daily work, and my clients as teachers, that I learned the commonalities that lie beneath the thin coat of "ego armor" linking us all together with each other, our world, and our vast universe. My observations have clearly convinced me that there is indeed a "pure wholism" that stretches far beyond Madison Avenue ad campaigns, and far beyond any trendy interpretations. It is a wholism that manifests as the subtle, limitless, unseen, yet undeniable power that governs and determines the ebb and flow of all life energy exchange, within, without, and between all of life as we know it. It is, I believe, when we come to better understand this marriage between physics and nature that we will open the door to the greatest healing potential of all.

We must first begin with subtraction, not addition, with surrender, not conquest. We are a culture, if not a world, that is victimized by our own obsessive-compulsive, "bigger, better, more" indoctrination. Advancing human progress, ever driven by ego, never seemed to take nature into consideration. Seldom throughout history have we taken the time to question whether or not human progress was in the best interest of our own truer inner nature or Mother Nature. Growth has always implied a progressive, self-serving, linear step forward without consideration of long-term effects or nature's approval.

Even today we are just beginning to see that progress, born of short-sighted vision, can have disastrously negative long-term repercussions. Too many industrial advances have meant too much pollution; too many insecticides have meant too much cancer; too many unnatural foods have meant too much illness; too much coastal development has meant too much instability of coastal terrain; too many air conditioners have meant too much ozone deterioration; too many medicines and food supplements have meant too many side effects; too much of the "good life" has meant too many unhealthy added pounds; too much sudden change has meant too much emotional insecurity; too much emotional repression has meant too much addiction; and on, and on. . . .

The power of nature is constantly moving about and around us as well as within us and always has the last word. We need only to look back at our grandparents and our great-grandparents to see a world that was still alive with this awareness. They understood creature habits, the changing seasons, and the nuances of nature's ways far better than we. They felt when the weather was about to change; they knew how to heal many of their own wounds and care for their land that it might return bountiful providence. They upheld the centrality of the family. They lived a much simpler, more natural life. The more I searched and studied, the more I became aware that our ancestors possessed an understanding of the powers and ways of nature that we somehow tragically lost somewhere along the way in our unnatural evolution. Our wholesale replacement of art with science, of nature with technology, represents what I call de-evolution or reverse evolution. Yet there remains an innate treasure lost somewhere deep within the confused de-evolved spirits of all of us. The most important healing gifts I can share with you are a shovel, a treasure map, and the inspiration to start digging your way to that treasure within.

The Wu Way is my healing gift–a shovel, treasure map, and inspiration–to you all. It is my attempt to reacquaint you with true universal whole-ism, so that you may take it from a philosophical, abstract concept to a more integrated, concrete, functional daily practice in your life, facilitating your great wholistic wellness and healing potential. It is my wish that you find the way home to your innate natural healing self, the "silent partner" that lies within. For this "silent partner" is attached to the universal system of perfection where limitless healing potential resides.

Throughout my endless research and study, I am continually impressed by the ancient Taoists' understanding of wholism. While many ancient cultures exhibit a wonderful understanding of nature and universal "whole-ism," the Taoists and their concept of "Wu Wei" (not forcing things) seemed to take whole-ism to another level. The Taoists felt that nature, with its order and subtle laws existing within and around us, was indeed perfect. And through the practice of "Wu Wei," they believed that man, in spite of his ego, could have consummate wellness simply by not interfering with nature. In *The Wu Way* I try to expand on this ancient concept by taking it from philosophy to practice as a contemporary healing guide.

With every person I counsel I see just how complex systemic disease and its causal root systems have become. I see from one person to the next how similar all our pains and obstacles, our fears, anxieties, and grievances are. I sense from each and every person just how out of sync we are with ourselves, our families, our fellow human beings, our jobs, our ailing bodies, and, in effect, our world. As an honored and humbled observer from the world of healing, I have come to understand the vital importance of self-responsibility in the healing process, for we must raise the will to unearth the de-evolutionary roots of destruction and at last sow the seeds of true healing.

The Wu Way is a guide to aid you in the acceptance of that responsibility, and the implementation of a more functional natural life as a basis for a more comprehensive personal and global healing. Though *The Wu Way* is thorough in its presentation of nutrition and dietary recommendations, it is not another "holistic" fad diet book. Thorough also in its recommendations for psychological and emotional healing, it is not another New Age self-help psychology book. And though equally thorough in its suggestions for spiritual healing, it is not in any way intended to be mistaken as another contemporary transcendental psycho-spiritual philosophy book. *The Wu Way* is the result of a culmination of my deductive observations and my innermost senses arriving at what I feel is the missing link to a more natural, whole, healthy existence.

The Wu Way presents an applied "wholism" which represents a vital missing link to profound, lasting healing. May it help put you back together with your body, your mind, your spirit, your fellow man, your world, your universe, and your God.

Mark Dana Mincolla, Ph.D.

1

Wu Wei

One thousand five hundred years before the birth of Christ, a people in North Central China known as the Shang prospered along the Yellow River. About 1100 B.C. the neighboring Chau people, who ultimately became the longest reigning dynasty in Chinese history, conquered the Shang. These two cultures blended together to form the Chan Dynasty, which contributed some of the greatest philosophical thinkers the world would ever know. Confucius, Chang Chao, Mo Ti, Mercius, and Shang Yang, to name a few, made contributions of brilliance and simplicity that remain timeless. It was also during this period that Lao Tze (640 B.C.), the founder of Taoism, and the Buddha (557 B.C.) were born. Specifically, it is with the birth of Taoism that the systematic conceptualization of universal duality (or Yin and Yang), was introduced. For the first time in history a civilization had cross-referenced the interrelationship of all things "between heaven and Earth"–Yin representing one group of universal elements as the shade on the north side of the hill, or all that is cold, dark, negative, and expansive, and Yang representing all those universal elements as the Sun on the south side of the hill, or all that is warm, light, positive, and contractive. Taoism was among the earliest philosophies that personified interconnectedness.

Taoism, or the "Tao," sometimes difficult for the Western mind to understand, has been described in many ways. The "flow of nature," the "way," and even God, or the way of the Father, have been used to describe the Tao. The Tao, a philosophy, is considered transcendental by some and actually religious by others. But most importantly the Tao represents the subtle perfection and order of the world and the universe which remain hidden to the human ego. The Tao intimates what the Chinese refer to as the "Implicit Order" or what the Buddhists call the "right way" or "right living," the art of living without forcing things. These thoughts intimate a natural path of understanding and living life which is diametrically opposed to the destructive path of the human ego. To further clarify, modern man has clearly chosen the path against the Tao, and eventualities or side effects from the path chosen are at the root of our obvious demise. The Tao represents a human attempt toward understanding and compliance with nature that offers an alternative to our collision course with disaster.

"In order to obtain the virtue of natural living man must surrender to nature. It will not come to him automatically. Though masculine, he must learn to deny himself and let the way be his way."[1] The Tao teaches that non-action represents man's only hope for true healthy prosperity on Earth. This non-action is referred to as "Wu Wei" (woo-way), literally translated to mean "not forcing things," or as I like to say, "The less man's ego does, the more nature will do through him." Nature is always attempting to work harmoniously in and around us. Modern man has chosen to overrule this natural harmonious process with the desires of his ego through his ever, expanding intellect. Wu Wei is not simply understood by intellect alone, it is a philosophy that must be sensed by the human heart and spirit.

---

[1]Lao Tzu, *The Way of Life*, (New York: R.B. Blakney, New Amer. Library, 1955), p. 44.

True now as it has been since the beginning of man's evolution on planet Earth, there are but two paths—the path of nature or the path of the human ego. I see it as the key to human survival as we approach the second millennium A.D. Modern man has all too often chosen the path of the human ego, where the priority is one of personal gratification, with little regard for the true nature of self and world or the ensuing consequences. But the signs, which are everywhere, point to the fact that the path of popular choice is finite and running out of road right before our eyes. This is clearly a critical time for the nature within and around mankind. As the planet goes, so go we. The Wu Wei reminds us that we are symbiotically interdependent, in a whole-istic tapestry, with the whole of our planet.

The Earth has existed for 4.6 billion years, the evolution of life on Planet Earth thriving and enduring for 2 billion years. Fish have evolved for 450 million years, amphibians for 360 million, reptiles for 300 million, mammals for 180, birds for 140 million, plants and vegetation for 2 billion years. Mother Earth and all her perfection and universal order continued to thrive naturally in accordance with the egoless dictates of "Implicit Order." This was Wu Wei. There were no egos to rise up against the natural order. Less than a million years ago man joined in this evolutionary dance, more specialized, more intelligent than any of his partners, but not without limitations. The greatest limitation of all would come at the hands of his own expanded ego that would one day foster the illusory perception of limitlessness. At last, after two billion years of evolution, there was a force capable of upsetting Wu Wei.

Dr. Noel Brown, a noted Ph.D. in International Law and Relations from Yale University, is highly respected for his views on the current dilemma of global environmental de-evolution. In a July 1990 interview with *M Magazine* Dr. Brown stated: "If present trends continue and we did nothing, I envision a semi-Hobbesian world where life would be miserable, nasty, brutish and short." He goes on to say that "the next ten years could make all the difference. The decade of the 90s, less than 4,000 days, is the last window of opportunity to turn the tide against environmental degradation. Nothing short of total mobilization of all sectors of society will be necessary." Brown says that "the most threatening enemy is global warming, caused by burning fossil fuels, using chlorofluorocarbons and nitrogen oxides, and deforestation." His description of global warming takes on Old Testament severity: "A significant rise in sea level will wipe out all our sea coasts; countries like Bangladesh will lose about 40 percent of their territory; some islands will disappear; salt water will contaminate fresh water tables; the atmosphere will become energy retentive, causing an increase in killer tornados, cyclones and hurricanes; vegetation will shift to undamaged areas, bringing with it insects that have long since been considered wiped out. The issues are unprecedented in human experience."[2]

The global warming theory represents a systemic de-evolutionary spiral, proving once again that one fundamental violation of natural law detonates a shock wave of endless chain reactions. One such aspect seldom mentioned, but worth noting here, is the breakdown of the Earth's protective electromagnetic force field. Many now believe that as we destroy the protective ozone layer with environmental pollutants, we also break down the Earth's magnetosphere. The magnetosphere is like a magnetic umbrella around the Earth, loaded with electrified particle fields in two concentric zones called the Van Allen belts, designed to both shield the Earth and hold it in proper gravitational suspension. Likened to cutting the strings on a marionette, disrupting these electromagnetic support grids with ozone destruction, the Earth's posture continues to "hunch" or "tilt" to one side, which, if it were to continue could set off catastrophic chain reactions never before thought possible. Mystics and prophets like Edgar Cayce, who foretold of the Earth's shifting axis, were considered absurd by most,

---

[2]*M Magazine*, (July 1990), p. 56 ff.

especially the scientific community. It wasn't until the early 1970s that the Naval Observatory began tracking and confirming the Earth's shift. The anticipated shift is estimated to be no more than 2 percent by some, while others predict it to be as much as 20 percent, enough to annihilate approximately one-fourth to one-third of the Earth's current population. Many theorize it is this shift in axis that causes flooding in some parts of the world and droughts in others, almost like a tilted glass of water with most of the water on one side of the glass while the other side remains empty and dry. The shift is being blamed by many for all our recent bizarre weather changes: hurricanes, Earthquakes, tornados, re-activated volcanos, famines, droughts, floods, and warm northern winters.

Was there a turn in the road or was mankind's turn from nature a gradual de-evolutionary process? Does it matter? All that does matter now is that we acknowledge the cold reality that has come full circle. We never really had the power to separate from nature. It is as if man was taken for a walk on a very, very long leash and decided to roam far from his master. The farther he roamed, the more he reinforced the illusion that he was free to roam farther still. At last man is at the end of the leash, and nature with her undeniable laws, reminds us she is, as always, an omnipotent reflection of "the way" that subtly yet profoundly compels adherence from all that lives. Man has at last followed the path of his own ego to the point where he now threatens to end his walk with nature.

The very Earth that grounds our feet and supports our life is being indiscriminately raped. "Every six hours we lose a piece of tropical rain forest the size of Boston. In effect, we lose a piece of Mother Earth at the rate of ten city blocks or 26 acres per minute. At the current rate, by the year 2081 deforestation of Planet Earth will be complete."[3] This loss is especially

---

[3] Information obtained from Franklin Park Zoo Research Team, Dorchester, MA, adapted from the Traveling Smithsonian Rainforest Exhibit, Washington, D.C.

disconcerting because tropical rain forests house half of all Earth's life. In fact each year one hundred species of animal life are lost by Mother Earth forever, extinction brought on by deforestation.

According to the Boston Franklin Park Zoo's Research Team, "By 1987 the world's population reached 5 billion and is currently growing at a rate of 100 million per year; 90 percent of the projected increases will take place in tropical Africa, Asia and Latin America where most of the remaining rain forests are. For man's first one million years he was a hunter; he then turned to farming for his livelihood. Since the beginning of his farming days, man has become a very territorial animal which he remains to this day. So, as these tropical zones increase in population, man will continue to lay claim to farming land most of which will continue to be tropical rain forests. Surprisingly, as many as 50-90% of all rural households in these regions are legally landless; the best agricultural farmland in the tropics is owned by a wealthy few."[4] Man, the most recent invitee to the dance of life, is most assuredly out of step with the Wu Wei, for as we can clearly see, insensitivity and disregard for the way of nature is unbounded. Our de-evolution from nature has affected the quality of our lives in all ways. We have divorced ourselves from nature's ways both within and without, but no greater sin has resulted from this madness than the indiscriminate desecration of the air and water so vital to our survival and the survival of our planet.

Isaac Asimov tells us: "Currently there are about 5,100,000,000,000,000 metric tons of noxious gases in our atmosphere, most of which has arisen from our own pollution. Since 1900, for instance, the carbon dioxide content of the atmosphere has risen 0.029%. In the past 100 years, man has added 325 billion tons of carbon dioxide to the Earth's atmosphere, and it is estimated that by the year 2000, the concentration may reach 0.038%, or an increase of some 30% in this century. This is the result, at least in part,

---

[4] ibid.

of the burning of fossil fuels, though it may also be due in part to the retreat of the forests that are more efficient as carbon dioxide absorbers than are other forms of vegetation."[5]

"It does not take much of an increase in the carbon dioxide concentration to intensify the greenhouse effect appreciably. The average temperature of the Earth could be one Celsius degree higher in 2000 than in 1900 because of the added carbon dioxide."[6] Asimov goes on to warn: "If we proceed to burn all the coal and oil available in the Earth's ground, the temperature would rise 7°C, enough to melt all the ice on Earth. If all the ice on Earth were to melt, the seas would elevate 70 meters or 230 feet, submerging New York and rising to the 25th story of the Empire State Building."[7]

We have nearly destroyed all the Earth's water as well. The ocean, which makes up 70 percent of the Earth's surface, is the recipient of three million metric tons of ship litter, five million tons of auto waste, and fifty million tons of sewerage per year from the United States alone. "The Earth's fresh water supply is only 2.7% of the Earth's total water supply, most of which is in solid ice form in the polar regions, not directly useful. In addition, a major portion of the 2.7% is untapped ground water, yet undiscovered, or hard to get at. The best supply is surface fresh water such as can be found in lakes, ponds, and rivers only equalling a mere 0.015% of the Earth's total water supply."[8] The pollution of our precious water supply comes from a great many sources: radioactive wastes from nuclear reactors, hospitals, laboratories, domestic waste water from urban America, chemical factory wastes, fallout from nuclear explosions, and chemical insecticides that run off into surface water sources

---

[5] Isaac Asimov, *A Choice of Catastrophes*, (New York: Simon & Schuster, 1979) p. 301.

[6] Isaac Asimov, *The Ends of The Earth*, (New York: Weybright & Tavey, 1975) p. 319.

[7] ibid., p. 346.

[8] ibid., p. 304.

and, carried by rain water, penetrate into deep ground water supplies. Rain water, often referred to as "acid rain," is water that has a pH below the normal 5.6 because of all the chemical contaminants absorbed. The most predominant acid rain pollutants are sulfur dioxide from coal-fired plants and nitrogen oxide, much of which comes from auto exhausts. America sends so much acid rain northward to Canada each year that "Canadian officials estimate that in the next 20 years 48,000 Canadian lakes will be rendered lifeless."[9]

Most of the sources of the water pollution are so chemically stable that they do not break down, but continue to build up and store in an accumulative manner. We have chosen our path, the path of technology and economic progress, without regard for the long-term ramifications. By the time big business stalls the environmentalists with their lobbying power and the legislative process slowly stumbles through its appeals and calls for scientific evidence, it is simply too late. As long as we continue to lack common sense and sensitivity, the entire planet and most of its inhabitants will continue on a course destined for further de-evolutionary chaos.

Internationally renowned environmentalist and author David Attenborough suggests that we hold the key not only to our own future, but to the future of all living creatures we share the Earth with, as well. Early man had this innate appreciation for he had not yet developed his ego to the point where he could delude himself into thinking he could circumvent the dictates of nature. The Wu Wei has two options but only one choice: nature's way or the way of the human ego. Until now we've chosen to feed our desires while destroying both the Earth and ourselves with an utter disregard for nature. We can continue to violate nature in the name of progress, but not without devastating consequences. For example, we must accept the

---

[9] Ralph Nader, Ronald Brownstein, John Richard, *Who's Poisoning America? Corporate Polluters and Their Victims in the Chemical Age*, (San Francisco: Nader and Sierra Club, 1981) p. 46.

fact that merely "two thousand of the Earth's 30 million animal species are currently considered safe from extinction. Currently, we are losing 1,000 animal species each year to the de-evolutionary spiral."[10]

We might liken the ego path or lost way to a motorized boat and the universal path or Wu Wei to a sailboat. The motorboat travels swiftly and powerfully, obeying the ego dictates of human desire and ingenuity, with little restriction by high seas or still, windless conditions. The sailboat, on the other hand, relies on the dictates of nature. The boat may sail only when the conditions are right. This is Wu Wei. When there is wind, we sail. When there is not, we wait until there is. We don't impose ourselves. This patience and compliance rewards the cooperative sailor with cleaner water and cleaner air. Harmony is the reward for compliance with nature. That is what this book is all about. It is my fervent wish to inspire and implore the reader to navigate his way through life more harmoniously; but to do so, there must first be a willingness to expand personal higher consciousness and good conscience to better understand and respect the concept of universal interconnectedness. We must look beyond the bias and limitation imposed by our contemporaary western culture. We must be willing to think from micro to macro. We must broaden our restricted horizons beyond the limitations imposed by ego-driven gratification to a more complete conceptual understanding of the universal wholism to which we are bound.

All and everything, animate and inanimate, even man, are by-products of the universe, subject to its laws and dictates. One basic conceptual universal law reminds us that in a domain limited by time and space, such as human life on Earth, all life is finite and linear. There is a beginning, a middle, an end. In Taoistic philosophical terms there is a natural sequence of contraction, expansion, and release. This

---

[10] WWF Special Report #4, (Gland, Switzerland: Jan. 1989).

"Implicit Order"–the hidden order throughout the universe, inescapable and unavoidable in all things–is in line with natural evolution. The Wu Wei is this natural evolution.

Primitive and ancient civilizations expressed their reverence for this "Implicit Order" by compliance with nature's dictates. Man, far less developed and therefore far less motivated by his ego, was in awe of nature. Nature was his god. Though still a part of him, it represented that which was greater than he. He knew well that compliance with this great force meant a more harmonious existence. As time moved on, man became aware that through the development and assertion of his ego, he could defy nature by attempting to provide himself with greater material pleasure and thus redefine materialism as his new god. Eventually, industrialization and technology would prove to be the messiahs that would one day deliver him from the governing hand of nature to his material diety. Now it appears that he has come to the end of an evolutionary cycle and reached a point of de-evolution, where his self-serving ego draws nearer its final manifestation of disregard for universal "Implicit Order."

One can easily see unmistakable signs of cyclical evolutionary termination at hand, not only for our fellow evolutionary dance partners (nature), but for ourselves. All the circumstances are right. Replacing nature with materialism has been costly. Though we have gained much through material and technological advancement, the losses from the calamitous, spiraling, unnatural side effects will soon force a halt to our rebellious existence. Our world and its inhabitants are dying a slow, agonizing death as the result of our choice to forego harmonious compliance with nature. The result of this can be seen in the current socio-environmental de-evolution which has reached a scope and magnitude of unprecedented proportions.

We are experiencing a dramatic world population explosion, primarily in coastal, industrial cities with overcrowding that fuels increasingly violent and neurotic human behavior. Such overcrowding, along with emphasis on production and competition, has left in its wake a world full of losers, for not everyone can succeed amidst the pressures of such a demanding, competitive, overpopulated world. As the casualty list of have-nots and drop-outs continues to grow, so, too, does the demand for an underground culture. Such escalating pressures bring drugs-for-profit into our upper middle class workplaces and school yards and sex-for-profit into suburbs and college campuses, scourges previously restricted to small deviant subcultures.

Scientific and technological advances have accelerated beyond our ability to comprehend or make safe use of them. What guarantees do we have against nuclear accidents? Or against increasing cancer rates due to the more than two thousand food additives that go into our foods each day? What will we learn of long-term exposure to microwaves and color television radiation or of the industrial pollution that currently contaminates our precious air and water? What of the climatic changes that are a direct result of our environmental and technological disregard?

We have clearly evolved from our once cooperative venture with nature. We are currently in a state of de-evolution. In the words of Yatri: "Enough cultural and technological upheaval currently exists to detonate the de-evolutionary bomb creating secondary chain reactions amongst themselves, much like the catalysts in a dissipative structure at a threshold."[11]

It is my foremost intention to inspire and implore active concern, for I believe an apocalypse lies in the balance of our fading sensitivity and our anomic inactivism. Currently in our world, scientifically unconfirmed crises require initial research and documentation prior to any extensive investments of time and money. Such sequential screening is ingrained in our culture, yet the impending nature of our current de-evolutionary crisis leaves us little time for such consternation. Our

---

[11] Yatri, *Unknown Man*, (New York/London: Simon & Schuster, 1988) p. 236.

11

culture embraces the analytical, the rational, the digital–explicit reductionist behavior.

This is why I am certain that many who read this book will ask "Where is the proof?". . . "How do you know this world is falling apart?". . ."What studies have been conducted to support your argument that we have come to the end of a cycle, or that we have de-evolved as the result of having lost sight of these metaphorical natural laws that you speak of?" I have great reservations regarding the establishment's tainted use of the scientific process in such matters. In 1989, Cable Network News reported that as much as 75 percent of all scientific research was paid "science-for-profit" research. As my father told me long ago, "Figures don't lie, but liars figure." Furthermore, how many years of advanced scientific study went into confirming the effects of nuclear exposure before U.S. soldiers were exposed to the great Nevada nuclear test site experiments in the 1950s? How much study went into cancer-causing cyclamates before they were allowed to go on the shelf? How many lives were lost? More important than all of this, what ever happened to natural, innate human awareness? Whatever became of the natural, common sense and sensitivity that once would have instinctively rejected such destructive de-evolutionary notions? My final question to the analytical sequentialist is simply this: If we are not de-evolving as separatists from nature from our own existential selves doomed at the hands of our own egos, do we have the luxury of time to confirm it by scientific study? I think not.

If all macro and micro sickness traces back to disharmony, and if this de-evolutionary sickness that I sense in my heart is real, then it has come about as the result of disharmony in many generations of humans–disharmony between soul and ego, nature and man. Man's continuing de-evolution is witnessed clearly in the loss of the intuitive to the analytical, of the existential to the reductionist, of sensitivity to insensitivity, of common sense to intellectualism, of higher conscience to ego;

of trust to fear, of the intuitive to the scientific, of the innate nature in man to the addictive illusion of material power fueled by his ego.

The healthy, natural evolution of an entire planet must first begin in the hearts and minds of individual human beings. To change outcomes, we must change our behavior. To change our behavior we must change our thoughts. To change our thoughts we must change our perceptions. In order for our perceptions to emanate from a higher source we must strive to gain access to our higher selves, i.e., the Wu Way suggests that we identify with our higher consciousness by tuning into our conscience; strive to commit ourselves to this higher consciousness; reinforce our commitment to good conscience on a day-to-day basis unconditionally. This alignment with higher consciousness represents the first step on the journey back to our natural self. The natural self is the healer within, awaiting affirmation.

Just as these ideals reflect the philosophy of Wu Wei, they also represent the sole healing force within us capable of stemming the tide of de-evolution. As these changing values become reinforced, they will color all areas of life, like dye cast into water. When our higher consciousness emerges from this alliance with conscience, then our truer nature within will take the place of destructive ego desensitization and greed. Currently, our higher natural senses remain deep in slumber as inactivism, born of desensitization, continues to fuel our de-evolutionary transit.

With the development of our natural higher consciousness, it will at last become a priority to clean up our bodies, our minds, our spirits, our foods, our air, our water, and our planet. The Wu Way is intended to inspire and guide you through this macro and microcosmic transformation as it is broken down into the following three parts: The Unnatural Body followed by The Wu Way to a Natural Body, The Unnatural Mind followed by The Wu Way to The Natural Mind and The Unnatural Spirit followed by The Wu Way to The Natural Spirit. I feel the need to combine dynamism, impact *and* fact to both support the de-evolutionary premise and implore the reader to make a commitment to reconcile with nature. Finally, I want this book to be hopeful, offering a functional, healing approach to the reader confronted with the personal and planetary task of survival as the second millennium approaches.

Wu Way Solutions for Healing the Earth

This chapter makes it clear that our home, Mother Earth, and the very air and water necessary for our future survival are severely threatened. Just as with ourselves, we can no longer postpone the Earth's healing. The time to make an active commitment is clearly at hand. If the student of the Wu Way is prepared to act, they might first consider the further study of two enlightening books. One is a comprehensive environmentalist's bible entitled, *Our Earth, Ourselves,* authored by Ruth Caplan and the Staff of Environmental Action, published by Bantam Books, New York, 1990. The other is an abridged version of the same entitled, *Fifty Simple Things You Can Do To Save The Earth,* The Earthworks Group, Copyright 1989, Earthworks Press, Box 24, 1400 Shattuck Avenue, Berkeley, CA 94709. These books are complete with information to help the reader with Earth healing suggestions. They're both educational and solution-oriented works that bring the reader hopeful means of counteracting the effects of global warming, ozone loss, urban smog, toxic air emissions, acid rain, toxic landfills, nuclear destruction, and water pollution. These books stimulate awareness, challenge involvement, and give practical suggestions for each of us to heal the Earth in our daily lives. The Wu Way suggests that we turn hope into reality with our awareness of what is and our commitment to involvement. If we care to further our commitment, there are a number of powerful, active coalitions busy at work healing Mother Earth every day. (Note comprehensive selected list of National Groups with Regional and Local Affiliates).

And so I welcome you to the Wu Way. Read with your intuitive as well as your analytical mind. And if you are inspired to tears over what was, anger over what is, or fears of what will be, may you also be led to aspire toward a higher, more natural personal transformation. It is a time for change. The signs are there for us to see. May this book arouse your higher self as the spirit of change invites and embraces you, in your life's ever-unfolding evolution, back to the old way of the Wu Wei, to a new way with the Wu Way!

2

The Unnatural Body

The Forgotten Path

The Wu Way sees all things as interconnected, relevant parts of the whole. The noun "whole" means:

> To be uninjured, unbroken, unimpaired. Undivided; in one piece. Containing all its parts or elements; unitary system.[1]

Of all the living members of Planet Earth, past or present, modern man is the only creature with enough ego and daring to attempt to detach himself from the Darwinian wholism (nature) for which he is foreordained.

In the beginning, primitive man was forced to comply with the movement of the stars, the changing of the seasons, the phases of the moon, and the dictates of his climate. Our earliest ancestors were forced to cooperate with their environment, their world, their universe, and the analogous laws or limitations imposed upon them.

Whether charting a travel course, planting or harvesting crops, or selecting the materials for shelter and clothing suited for his environment, primitive man learned to harmonize with

---

[1] *Webster's College Dictionary,* ed. (New York: Random House, 1991), p. 521.

17

the natural way of things in order to survive. The earliest humans had an innate sense of true "wholism" with reverence for the awesome hand of nature, while undeniably interconnected with it. It is most important here to consider the term "dualism" in the same context with "wholism." Dualism is an esoteric term referring to the two basic natures of man: "real self" and "ego self." Clearly, primitive man was forced to function more from his real or natural self in order to cooperate with natural environmental forces greater than he. The ego self refers to the drive in man that seeks personal expression, regardless of long-term repercussions that may arise from violating natural law.

When balanced together and tempered by a higher awareness of natural law, ego self and real self represent "whole man." The Wu Way believes that modern man has disharmoniously evolved due to the predominance of his ego development. Obsessed with his compulsive drive for self-gratification and mastery, man would one day divorce his once perfect marriage with nature and ultimately engage himself on a technological crusade against the limitations imposed by natural law. Until recently it seemed as though he had beaten nature's system. He evolved *in spite of* his surroundings, not in humble cooperation with them. Once mankind was an inextricable part of the whole, organizationally tied into the life force. Having evolved from agrarian to industrial to higher left brain technological intelligence, rebelliously he set out to synthetically improve upon the basic "wholistic nature" to which he is undeniably bound.

Nature is not to be outdone; for clearly, her laws allow no dispensations and no exceptions to the rules. Currently, our evolving industrial-technological civilization views the laws of nature as a challenging set of limitations that must be overcome with the proper ingenuity, resources, and will. Yet, as human progress ignores natural law, or the conceptual acknowledgement of wholism, such progress carries with it a costly "cause" and "effect" syndrome that serves to reverse the natural evolutionary spiral. This de-evolutionary effect of our willful detachment from nature is increasingly evident as it continues to weave its way through every fiber in the tapestry of modern human life.

As aerosol sprays, microwave ovens, color TVs and food additives continue to solve many short-term day-to-day problems, they do so with increasing long-term risks to human life and the environment. The unnatural way begins with the exercise of man's "ego-will" to overcome the limitations imposed by nature with little regard for nature's laws. Nature, not man, will always have the last word, manifesting as a new set of repercussive limitations with continuing domino side effects. And as this happens, modern man will be tempted to exhibit additional exercise of will, again in spite of nature, making the systemic process of de-evolution even more interminable.

Every aspect of modern life is tainted with the poison of de-evolution. As evidence, our world, our air, our water, our entire macrocosm, if you will, continues to suffer from that insensitive disregard. De-evolution is a spreading cancer that first emanates from deep within the microcosm of the human mind. Consequently, our world within, our bodies and our spirits, remain victims of our own demise. The insensitive pollution of our bodies and minds are, in effect, synonymous with the pollution of our world. The disharmony between our minds and bodies initiates the endless discord. Our bodies, being of nature, need nature in order to endure. Natural food, pure water, clean air, and natural medicine have been and will always be essential to our survival. Yet our modern minds, now fully divorced from nature, including the nature of our own bodies, no longer know how to care for, maintain, or heal our de-evolved bodies. Our natural bodies have become prisoners to our unnatural minds. Our unnatural minds no longer house the spirit of the healer within.

The Retired Healer Within

Where our ancestors once held enough reverence for and understanding of nature to prevent illness and heal themselves naturally, we now seem lost. With unnatural living come unnatural consequences such as the lost art of prevention and true whole-ism.

Today at the first sign of symptoms, a patient will usually be issued a prescription for pharmaceutical drugs. Before long the initial symptoms are under control, only to be followed by an entirely new set of symptoms, or side effects brought on by the drugs. So the patient returns to the physician and receives a new set of recommendations designed to nullify the side effects brought on by the first. Soon our patient will most likely have a medicine chest that resembles a small pharmacy and a list of symptoms that grows ever longer.

Let us assume for a moment that a patient goes to the doctor complaining of severe headaches. Let us also say that the patient has a history of hypoglycemia or low blood sugar, a condition where the glucose or body "fuel" levels are often on empty, leaving the brain starved and giving rise to such brain and head symptoms as headaches, dizziness, even anxiety and depression. It has been clearly demonstrated that proper diet can help in controlling this condition. Understanding that the body attempts to prompt attention with these headaches, as a sort of alarm, would be consistent with wholism. On the other hand, if the same patient were experiencing headaches, he might be inclined to run off to the doctor in hot pursuit of a pharmaceutical prescription to deaden the nerve endings and thus end the "alarming" pain, only to find some time later that his hypoglycemic condition had progressively worsened.

It would have been far better for our sample patient to have "tuned in," not "tuned out." The headache was part of the natural body defense, or "doctor within," designed to get his attention with the intention of coercing compliance with his body's needs for whole natural support. His condition could be seen as systemic or wholistic, as it was both precipitated and predisposed by a set of pre-existing conditions, behaviors, and choices.

I recently had occasion to counsel a young successful plumbing contractor. He'd had a number of nagging complaints, and yet still needed convincing that his junk food laden diet was implicated. Instead of debating the issue, I asked him to picture himself purchasing an expensive piece of plumbing equipment, the kind sent with detailed maintenance instructions and a factory representative to make certain that both the operation and maintenance requirements are complied with and fully understood. "The machine," I pointed out to him, "was designed with specific needs and specs. There is simply no way under the sun that you would jeopardize such sensitive, valuable equipment with careless maintenance." I then took great pains to point out to him that the human body, clearly the most sensitive, high-performance machine known to man, with all its irreplaceable parts, was built with specific maintenance needs, based on a million years of evolution, not ten seconds of impulse. Yet every day our ego impulses direct us to synthetic "taste good, feel good" artificial foods that greatly upset the balance of our precious body machine. It seems our synthetic spirits have drifted too far from nature and too far from the natural needs of our bodies. It is for the sake of our synthetically exploited bodies that we need to encourage natural systems of health maintenance and healing such as those embraced by many cultures and civilizations that have preceded us.

As the nuances and complexities of a natural holistic system are more fully understood, they may then be applied as an effective, preventive, and therapeutic model of drugless healing. Any functional application of prevention must first begin with knowledge of an effective, natural system. Knowledge of a natural system begins with the awakening of our slumbering, innate sense of natural law.

Natural Law Forgotten

As our innate awareness of whole-ism and natural law gradually awaken, we can no longer ignore the devastating magnitude of our current de-evolutionary crisis. We must acknowledge that our greatest hope lies with our willingness to reconnect somehow to the whole, to reacquaint with the more literal translation of wholism, and to recommit to the process of natural evolution.

Alliance with nature begins with a commitment to "common sense," "good conscience," and "wholism," for the interconnectedness of all things remains a most basic undeniable absolute. Many ancient civilizations considered such issues paramount in the pursuit of wellness and consummate purposefulness. Ancient Chinese sages established Seven Infinite Laws of the Universe which are listed below along with the Wu Way's extrapolations (*):

(1) That which has a front has a back.
*Everything that is in its natural state is complete.
(2) That which has a beginning has an end.
*Finite can never be infinite, earthly perfection is an illusion.
(3) There is nothing identical in the universe.
*Everything is unique.
(4) The bigger the front, the bigger the back.
*Reality can not be hidden.
(5) All antagonisms are complementary.
*Opposition provides tension for growth.
(6) All antagonisms are also opposites.
*The tension from opposition remains forever necessary.
(7) Opposites are the two arms of infinity, absolute oneness, or God.
*Extremes ultimately lead us to balance.

These may seem oversimplified or contradictory in some cases, but, in fact, they are applicable to any and all situations. More important, they represent a human striving to understand

and cooperate with the universal system. They represent a simplicity that reflects a common sense and a greater sensitivity. We no longer understand systemic process; we are simply not so inclined any more. And no longer do we place premiums on common sense, conscience, or sensitivity. We are becoming more desensitized, anomic, and egocentric with every ensuing generation. We are "turned off" and "tuned out" just like the earlier general reference to our symptom-riddled patient. Had he cooperated with the warning systems previously triggered by his body and mind in response to the initial symptoms of his disharmonious condition, his illness might not have progressed.

It is Dr. Samuel Hahnemann, the founder of homeopathy, (a system of natural medicine) who first taught that miasms (etiological origins) lie at the root of all chronic disease. Miasms may remain dormant for years and even generations but eventually can flare up to cause chronic or acute illnesses. Their viral or bacterial traits are contained within cells which means a miasm is not necessarily a disease but has potential for disease. Although Dr. Hahnemann identified three inherited miasms, we now accept that there are seven. They are:

(1) Psora–the mother of all disease; a rythmic imbalance between body and mind.

(2) Syphilitic/Gonorrheic–sexual transmission with destructive effect on all tissues and bones.

(3) Sycotic–sexual transmission (partly gonorrehic) causing deposits, congestion, and tumor formations. Disorders are found in the pelvic and sexual areas as well as skin, digestive, respiratory, and urinary tract.

(4) Tubercular–from tuberculosis causing respiratory, circulatory, urinary, and digestive disorders.

(5) Radiational–from background radiational exposure causing allergies, skin disorders, cancer, endocrine system deterioration, weakening of bone tissues, anemia, arthritis, etc.

(6) Toxic Metallic–from lead, mercury, radium, arsenic, carbon, aluminum, and fluoride causing allergies, hair loss, fluid retention, poor calcium assimilation, viral susceptibility.

(7) Petrochemical–from petroleum and chemically based products causing diabetes, infertility, miscarriages, premature graying of hair, muscle degenerative disease, hair loss.

There are 38,000 diseases occurring from one or more of the seven inherited miasms. Even though we are constantly inundated with new symptoms there are still the same number of organs that can be affected. Lastly, all disease manifests in one or more of the following sub-sources:

(1) Chemical–toxemia, infections, chemical imbalance.

(2) Mechanical–spinal lesions, trauma, pressure.

(3) Psycho-somatic–incoordination between the mental and physical.

(4) Environmental–atmosphere, occupation, social factors.

Symptoms are a kind of "body talk" designed to work in our favor. Dr. Edward Bach, founder of Bach Homeopathic Medicines said, "Disease is not an evil, but a blessing in disguise whose purpose is solely and purely corrective." One pain for the greater good of one's total wellness, or as the ancient Chinese described in the fifth infinite law of the universe: all antagonisms are complementary. We have much to gain from this broader view provided by wholistic systems that regard both disease and wellness as synergistic antagonisms. Antagonisms co-exist as inseparable parts of one great, all-inclusive whole, just as night ushers in day, just as death gives birth to new life.

We need to have a better understanding of the wholistic, complementary dynamic of these antagonisms if we are to deal more successfully with disease (disharmony). It is also imperative that we strive toward this understanding without delay, for the de-evolutionary cycle is speeding up at an alarming rate. The Wu Way believes our current total reliance on non-wholistic (unnatural), technological healing strategies will only continue to fall short of the mark. According to the Centers for Disease Control, in 1987 AIDS-related deaths exceeded 11,000 and combined cancers for that same period exceeded 400,000. At the same time, Senate committee statistics indicate that one in three men and one in six women can expect to die from heart disease before the age of sixty.

Our ailing culture remains starved for answers, yet we continue to look in all the wrong places. We are too willing to support and finance research in the areas of immune depletion in desperate hope of new miracle drugs or any vital information that could perhaps save human life. We human beings all share in the same dream for a long, healthy, prosperous existence in which we are given every opportunity to live our lives to the fullest without the curse of untimely death. Currently, most of us defer responsibility, left only to hope and pray that we might be deserving of a kinder fate, almost as if we were puppets on a string, powerless but for the grace of God and our "miraculous" health care system.

Why do we continue to reject the notion of our own self-empowerment? Why are we so willing to defer personal responsibility to researchers and doctors? How many of our own lives could we save with the employment of a true wholistic preventive system? How much unnatural, untimely disease could be avoided? When we see "effect," wholistically we see "cause." When we see the causes, we begin seeing probability factors which tie into a myriad of behavioral variables such as stress, diet, emotions, environment, etc. Before long we can see how nothing happens by accident and how simple applications of common sense and discipline alone may just be the greatest miracle drugs ever to save human life. Even now someone is experiencing preventable, untimely death, and though there will be many asking why, too few will ever really be inclined to sift through the miasms in order to stem the tide of such fatalism.

The Wu Way implores us to adopt a natural healing system which encourages our involvement. A system founded on the principle of complementation of all antagonisms, from disease and wellness, to life and death. When one embraces such a philosophy, he is far better equipped to live wholly through the natural living and dying process. Many studies now suggest that in the long run patient involvement alone drastically improves a patient's chances for recovery and survival. Where there is affirmation of self-empowerment, there is a healing "spirit" or "life force" within that body. Self-empowerment is a by-product of, and a vital step toward, true wellness. Nietzsche, in *Thus Spake Zarathustra,* imagined a future race of humans who had prioritized the pursuit of health naturally, through self-discipline and self-awareness. He referred to these denizens as "the last men" and said, "They have their little pleasure by day and their little pleasure for the night: but they respect health."[2] They waited not for miracles nor miracle cures. They assumed responsibility for their health by ideologically reconnecting with the dictates of natural law. Natural law dictates that the strong heart endures, so they strengthened the heart through exercise. Nature tells us that a strong mind makes for a strong body, so they adopted the power of positive thinking. Perhaps it was a prophetic air with which Nietzsche named these healthy "last inhabitants"[3] of future Earth.

Natural Law and Immuno-Suppressive Disease Prevention

To shift the paradigm from separatistic, fatalistic disease arising from egoism and de-evolution, we must apply our awareness of natural law to disease prevention strategies. A good place to begin would be in expanding our existing knowledge of

---

[2] Michael Ignatieff, "Modern Dying," *The New Republic,* December 26, 1988, (199), pp. 28-33.

[3] ibid.

nutrition and human immunity. I am not suggesting that each of us go out and enroll in some graduate level courses on immunology or nutrition. That is hardly necessary. But I am suggesting that we establish a basic understanding of our immune properties, nutritional needs, and their relationship to human wellness. There is growing interest in stepping up AIDS and cancer awareness among well-intentioned, intelligent people the world over. Yet, how many of us can even identify the major parts of our own immune systems?

It is unconscionable that a nation supposedly so committed to AIDS and cancer issues spends all of its time canvassing for research dollars and all of its money on studying the viruses, while not a word is spoken about supporting and maintaining our immune systems. It is as if we are spending all of our time spying on and studying the habits of the enemy and absolutely no time on reinforcing the walls of our own precious immune fortress. It is puzzling to me why we are not teaching immune awareness at a grade school level. We could make it simple, understandable, associative learning. One could envision "Pac-man" type antibody cells devouring dangerously invasive cancer and AIDS cells. Where are our priorities? The cynical viewpoint is that there is simply too much profit derived from the present approach and not enough profit to be gained from any immune awareness campaigns. Once again, it comes down to personal responsibility. When considering any effective model of wholistic health care, personal responsibility and adherence to natural law are most essential.

Our immune system is our first line of defense against all illness and disease. If we are to mount a formidable immune defense against invaders such as bacteria and viruses, this system must first be supported and enhanced. Each of us must discover, acknowledge, and expand our awareness of this vitally important disease-fighting protector within. There is so much controversy right now that we can no longer afford to comfortably sit back and be spoon-fed information by the healing establishment. There is much deception whenever there is so much at stake.

Recently I had the opportunity to listen to a nationally syndicated radio interview with internationally renowned molecular biologists/authors Drs. William O'Connor and Campbell Douglas. It was alarming, though enlightening, to hear these well-respected men of science discuss the all-too-real, sci-fi-like AIDS conspiracy theory they claimed to have uncovered. They went on to explain how the scientific community has, in fact, genetically engineered the AIDS virus through a process called "serial passaging," a means of integrating chromosomes from one virus to another and even one species to another. Dr. O'Connor explained how they can actually take the chromosomes from a human virus and integrate them with other chromosomes such as snake venom. They may then introduce the integrated chromosomes into the human system. Each time that human being is further exposed to that particular virus, his body will actually trigger a secretion of snake venom. This powerful imprinting carries a devastating potential, extending its powers far beyond the human immune capability. Viruses and bacteria integrated from one human to another or from one species to another leave the immune identification cells at a distinct disadvantage, which in turn renders aggressor cells incapable of fighting off this powerful genetically engineered enemy. This is precisely what Drs. O'Connor and Douglas theorize is happening at present. They feel strongly that science is playing god behind our backs with this serial passaging technique. What's more, they feel we're all being continually exposed to these engineered viruses and bacteria in a clandestine experimental fashion, the result being the steady increase of the AIDS infection, as well as infection from other immune-depleting viruses such as EBV, CMV (Cytomegalo Virus), mononucleosis, herpes, etc. Drs. O'Connor and Douglas then went on to point out that all of these viruses, including the AIDS virus, have the same characteristics, and are therefore, in fact, sufficiently communicated via saliva. Backing this up they stated there was ample documentation of numerous AIDS patients with no previous history of sexual relations or transfusions. They cited a specific example of one diabetic patient with no previous history of sexual experiences or blood transfusions who tested HIV positive. They are emphatically convinced that the present scientific community and medical community, as well as the government, are conspiring in efforts to squash this information.

Whether the above scenario is accurate or not, there are still a lot of hard questions we need to ask the health care system in regards to AIDS. Dr. Lorraine Day, orthopedic surgeon and author of *What The Government Isn't Telling You About AIDS*, informs us that the government's current "safe sex" posture is irresponsible and unsafe. According to Dr. Day, prophylactics have holes, the average size being .5 microns; the AIDS virus averages .1 micron; a micron being one millionth of a meter. While offering potential protection against pregnancy (sperm being 450 times larger that the AIDS virus) the prophylactic offers little or no protection against the spread of the HIV virus. Yet, our government continues to advocate the use of prophylactics for "safe sex." The Wu Way once again urges each of us to assume personal responsibility for the maintenance of our bodies, minds, and spirits. We can no longer rely on blindly entrusting our precious selves to the "father-protector" establishment. The government, the health care system, the food and advertising industry, and the scientific community are all, at this point in time, riddled with enough de-evolved, desensitized people whose twisted priorities operate in violation of our trust. Immune maintenance is ultimately a personal choice. Viruses and bacteria are plentiful. A "deathly white plague" lurks in the shadow of us all. In the balance, we will either recommit ourselves to the way of nature and universal order with a heightened sense of personal responsibility—or succumb.

We have to awaken the retired healer within, but before this awakening can occur we must first develop a more complete wholistic understanding of self in relation to nature. Any truly meaningful discussion of wellness must begin with wholism, and any truly meaningful discussion of wholism must begin with preventive nutrition and human immunity. Human immunity or wellness preservation, not unlike human disease, must be directed systemically to the body, mind, and spirit. There are immune functions and dysfunctions in each of these separate areas that ultimately stem from an array of pre-existing harmonies and disharmonies. The modern human immune system is rapidly deteriorating as a natural consequence of our disharmonious choice to de-evolve, physically, mentally, and spiritually. As we continue to drift farther from the laws of nature, our immune bodies suffer, our immune mental input grows more negative, and our human immune spirit hangs by a mere thread.

Nutrition and Immunity

Currently the average American consumes more than 130 pounds of sugar per year and 15 pounds of food additives. According to government statistics, 60 percent of our total caloric intake is composed of fat and sugar. In 1979, a Senate subcommittee reported that the American diet (which typically includes an overconsumption of saturated fat, cholesterol, sugar, salt, and alcohol) is related to six of the leading ten causes of death: heart disease, cancer, cerebrovascular disease, diabetes, arteriosclerosis, and cirrhosis of the liver. Dr. D. Mark Hegsted of the Harvard School of Public Health, in his subcommittee testimony statement, said:

> I wish to stress that there is a great deal of evidence and it continues to accumulate, which strongly implicates and, in some instances, proves that the major causes of death and disability in the United States are related to the diet we eat. I include coronary artery disease which accounts

for nearly half of the deaths in the United States, several of the most important forms of cancer, hypertension, diabetes and obesity as well as other chronic diseases.[4]

Today's highly processed foods are denatured and poor imitations of what healing, life-giving foods were intended to be. Food historians and anthropologists estimate that for the better part of a million years of human history almost 60-70 percent of the average human's total caloric intake consisted of crude, unrefined whole grains and their by-products. Wheat, corn, millet, oats, rice, barley, and rye were the staple foods of this entire planet. They could sustain life without requiring preservation or refrigeration and could be harvested in abundance on all continents. The remaining carbohydrates came from fruits and vegetables, which were, of course, indigenously, as well as seasonally, restricted. Meats were generally difficult and costly to obtain, making poultry, fish, beans, and legumes often the preferred choice of proteins.

Once again, we see how primitive man, being less technologically developed, had little choice but to comply with the dictates of his environment. However, this was often to his advantage in terms of disease prevention. He was less apt to have problems with colon-rectal cancer thanks to the high fiber from his whole grain diet. Also, he had little or no problem with cholesterol-related heart disease; again there was increased fiber intake, as well as very little available fatty meat and whole fatty dairy products.

A less obvious health benefit from early man's Darwinian existence was certainly greater efficiency of digestion. There is nothing more taxing on a digestive system than excessive food variety, density, and general overconsumption. The digestive system can be likened to a common laborer; the simpler the job the more efficient the productivity.

---

[4] *Dietary Goals For The United States,* Select Committee on Nutrition and Human Needs, United States Senate, Washington, DC, 12/77, p. 1.

With today's modern shipping, refrigeration, and technology in general, our overworked digestive systems are confronted with the difficult task of having to digest and assimilate foods from a variety of groups, not to mention from every corner of the globe. For a million years a body was not likely to have more than one or two foods per day, no more than five or six in a given week and almost always from within an indigenous radius of ten miles. Now, suddenly, we have a cornucopia of endless choices.

We must also keep in mind that digestion is highly specialized and requires specific enzymes to break down specific corresponding foods in order for nutrients to be made available for assimilation. There are one thousand enzymes within every cell in our body, with over eighty thousand total enzyme systems in all. These enzymes are protein molecules which act as catalysts that assist us in the breakdown of chemical bonds, or in this case foods. Not unlike the color of our eyes and hair, the development of these highly specialized digestive enzymes is genetically predetermined. For example, if for ten generations my progenitors were from a part of the world where wheat was the staple grain, there is a strong likelihood that I, too, will be equipped with the full compliment of digestive enzymes to facilitate proper digestion of wheat. With today's shrinking world and melting-pot of cultures, not to mention mass marketing of commercial food products, our digestive systems are clearly overworked, setting the stage for a broad spectrum of food intolerance (allergies). These food intolerances and their diverse symptomatology have become an all too common factor in the de-evolution of human health, ultimately affecting human immunology. We select our daily foods based largely on pleasure and convenience with near-limitless availability. We automatically assume that any food we eat is simply digested, leaving us with all the supportive nutrients, with the unusable residues simply exiting the body. However, proper food utilization is a very complex seven-step process:

(1) Ingestion;

(2) Digestion;

(3) Absorption;

(4) Transportation of nutrients;

(5) Respiration;

(6) Metabolism of nutrients; and

(7) Excretion of wastes.

This process drastically affects the physical and chemical interchanges that take place within all the cells of the body, which in turn affect every major system within the body, including the precious immune system, the fortress that protects and defends us from all disease.

Neurophysiologist David Horrobin of the Clinical Research Institute in Montreal maintains that a hormonelike biochemical, prostaglandin E, is a nutritional substance vitally important to healthy immune functioning. This Oxford University scientist feels strongly that it is only through diet that a person can stimulate immuno-effective T-cells. "By careful attention to diet," he declares, "it should be possible to activate T-lymphocyte function in a large number of diseases, including rheumatoid arthritis, various anti-immune diseases, multiple sclerosis, and cancer."[5]

Protein, one of the three major food components, has a profound influence on human immune function. Food proteins greatly influence antibodies, which are also major proteins that act in our behalf against disease agents such as viruses. These food proteins are derived from 28 amino acids, many of which provide immune antibody support, thus aiding disease prevention. Healthy, immune-supported diets should have a 2:1 ratio of lysine to arginine. Lysine is an amino acid protein component found in abundance in many foods such as

---

[5] Stephen Locke, M.D., and Douglas Colligan, *The Healer Within,* (New York: New American Library, 1986), p. 238.

poultry, fish, beans, and legumes. L-lysine is an immune-functioning, isolated, supplemental form of lysine that may be purchased at health food stores. L-lysine has been shown to halt the replication of certain immuno-suppressive viruses such as oral herpes. On the contrary, when foods such as peanuts, various nutritional yeasts, and corn are consumed in excess, their high content of agrinine (another amino acid), can actually suppress immunity and support virus replication. The delicate nutritional balance of these amino acids and, for that matter, all nutrients affects biochemistry, which in turn exerts a powerful influence on the human immune system.

Perhaps the most significant relationship between digestion and immunity, or nutrition and wellness, can be seen with the immune system's interaction with digestive residues of single-cell bacteria, which evolve from the sub-cellular 16-chain aerobiosis cycle. This 16-chain cycle begins with somatids followed by spores, double spores, and finally, the first bacterial form. These single-cell bacteria are capable of respiration, circulation, synthesis of new materials, breakdown of materials for energy, response to environment, reproduction, and excretion. Their survival and advancing development depend on a favorable environment. Ninety-nine percent of these single-cell bacteria are anaerobic, and proliferate in the large intestine, where, again based on conditions in the colon, they are either friend or foe, invasive or non-invasive. Favorable or unfavorable criteria are established in a number of ways. Digestive conditions are most favorable to the host when the bowel is clean from fibrous foods, and food selection does not include heavy, complex foods from *too many* food groups consumed in excess. However, today's accepted diet clearly runs contrary to this. According to well known medical expert Harvey Kellogg, M.D., "Of the twenty-two thousand operations I personally performed, I never found a single normal colon. And of the one hundred thousand performed under my jurisdiction, not over six percent were normal." Recently, one well known expert estimated that the average 50-year-old American withholds approximately 14 pounds of non-digested putrefying and fermenting fecal matter in the colon. The modern American diet provides a favorable condition for an invasive array of dangerous single-cell bacteria posing a very direct threat to our immune systems. Keeping in mind that the environment of the large intestine is at 98.6°F, consists of 57 percent water or vapor, and is largely anaerobic, it is clearly a dangerously unhealthy place to store any non-digested food residues, unless of course you're an invasive single-cell bacterium in need of housing!

The Primary Immune Checkpoint

Renowned scientist Dr. Gaston Naessens, referred to as the Galileo of the microscope for his invention of the revolutionary somatoscope (most powerful microscope in the world), discovered the pleomorphic (form changing) 16-chain cycle of aerobiosis which ultimately culminates with immune invasive fibrous thallus bacterial forms. These bacterial parasites which begin, as all of life does, with somatids or "tiny bodies," subcellular micro-organisms, ultimately have the power to invade human blood cells through advanced cell division. This, it is theorized by some experts, is where AIDS, cancer, and all serious immune scenarios actually begin. The cycle begins with somatids progressing to spores and double spores. Up to this point in the cycle, all is well. These first three stages are perfectly normal and, in fact, crucial in all healthy, living organisms. "Naessens found that if and when the immune system of an animal or human being has been weakened or de-stabilized, the normal three-stage cycle goes through thirteen more successive growth stages to make up a total of sixteen separate forms, each evolving into the next."[6] There are no immune implications until the next stage of this cycle,

---

[6] Christopher Bird, *The Trial and Persecution of Gaston Naessens,* (Tiburon, CA: H.J. Kramer, Inc., 1991), p. 9.

which is bacterial, followed by double bacterial forms, rod forms, bacterial forms with double spores, bacterial forms with granular double spores, microbial globular forms, bursting forms, yeast forms, ascopores, asci forms, mycelial forms, all concluding with rich milieu and fibrous thallus.[7]

For our purposes here, bacterial, yeast, and mycelial forms are where the most profound immune breakdown begins. The presence of these invasive single-cell microbes in the intestines, due primarily to modern diet, is of increasing immune significance. One of the more common forms, a single-cell fungus *Candida albicans*, proliferates in the large intestine and can easily advance itself on the aerobiosis cycle from a yeast to a dangerous mycelial fungal form. Once in a fungal form, it produces rhizomes—long, root-like structures that invasively penetrate intestinal mucousal walls. Once the gastrointestinal mucousal walls are infiltrated and broken down, this bacterial organism can gain entry into the bloodstream, finding its way into a variety of soft internal tissues, including the tissues of all the vital glands and organs of the body. There it can continue to reproduce, leaving in its wake recurring vaginal infections, stiff joints, chest pains, cystitis, and much more. What's worse, once the mycelial invader accesses the bloodstream, it may then continue cell division, advancing to the rich milieu cycle where potentially life-threatening immune disorders may, at last, begin their tragic assault on the host.

Antibiotic therapy is often the prescribed mode of treatment in this advanced scenario, and ironically often serves to further the problem in the long run. Broad-spectrum antibiotics not only kill off the invasive "bad" bacteria, but they are non-discriminating in their action and may kill off many protective microfloral "good" bacteria. The remaining "bad" surviving bacteria, as well as those that were safely infiltrated deep within tissue walls, are then free to re-colonize, restoring their

---

[7] ibid., p. 6, Figure 1.

strength in numbers far more swiftly than any of our immune system's protective "friendly" bacteria, thus opening the door to recurring cycles of infection.

A recent, especially alarming report shows that a high percentage of AIDS patients have previously had chronic Candida bacterial infections. According to a 1984 study from *The New England Journal of Medicine* by Nathan Clumeck, eight of fifteen African AIDS patients in a group with no history of homosexuality, blood product transfusions, intravenous drug abuse, or other underlying immuno-suppressive diseases, were diagnosed as having chronic *Candida albicans,* or polysystemic chronic candidiasis. The threat of this often overlooked and misunderstood syndrome must not be underestimated. As we now know, it represents an advancing immune invasion on the sixteen-stage microcycle. This is where the immunity war is constantly being waged full scale. The bacterial dilemma is the primary immune checkpoint. "But how," you may ask, "can this war be won; how can immunity be maintained at this vital immune checkpoint?" Soon after this bacterial immune checkpoint is infiltrated, there is usually a broadening of immune destabilization.

"Naessens found that this immune trauma is brought on by a host of reasons ranging from various forms of radiation or chemical pollution (which includes dietary, air, and water), to accidents, shocks, depressed psychological states and many more."[8] Even the healing establishment is beginning to recognize such correlating co-factors.

The Centers for Disease Control considers chronic Candida as one main criterion on its list of opportunistic diseases required to fit the case definition in the diagnosis of ARC (AIDS Related Condition) and AIDS (Acquired Immune Deficiency Syndrome). Present in the human body from birth to death, this yeast-like organism lives in the intestinal tract without aggra-

---

[8] ibid., p. 9.

vating symptoms until periods of acute stress or the immune system is suppressed. This precipitating immune-depleting condition may then be further exacerbated by such things as long-term use of antibiotics, oral contraceptives, excessive intake of fermented foods like pizza, beer, wine, vinegar, and soy sauces, as well as mold and fungal foods like peanuts, peanut butter, mushrooms, morels, and truffles. In addition, sweets and desserts abundant with processed sugars and starches create an acid pH in the large intestines which only serves to further this condition. Successful treatment is largely dietary, and requires one so diagnosed to avoid most of the aforementioned foods, at least for a given treatment period.

Based largely on the incredible work of Naessens, there is at last scientific evidence that a direct relationship exists between diet-related single-cell bacteria such as Candida and potentially life-threatening viruses such as AIDS and many cancer-type viruses. The Wu Way is in agreement with Naessens' conclusions that AIDS and cancer viruses are part of a systemic, sequential disease process originating with sub-cellular bacterial precursors which then become invasive immuno-suppressive bacteria. It is important to remember here that disease and wellness are separate but interrelated systems. As the fifth Infinite Law of the Universe reminds us, "all antagonisms are complementary." Though antagonistic pain, tension, and difficulty result from opposing the desires of our egos, compliance with our natural body needs will ultimately bring harmonious reward. Disease/dis-harmony stems from violation of Nature's law; wellness/harmony stems from cooperation with nature. We choose foods that please our desirous egos while disregarding the natural needs of our bodies. Sweets and highly processed carbohydrate dessert foods taste great even though they upset intestinal pH with extreme acidity. This toxic acid environment then supports invasive bacteria, which begin weakening our immune systems. This systemic immune breakdown may then be furthered by unnatural medicines like antibiotics, which help in the short-term by killing unfriendly bacteria but may perpetuate the problem in the long run with their destruction of our protective, friendly bacteria. (**Note:** If properly recommended by a trained and licensed physician, these and other pharmaceutical medicines may be of great benefit, and in some cases, can be of life saving importance.)

As this immune system turns over and over, more damage is sustained, until the 400-plus viruses that we host every day of our lives from birth to death impose a more profound impact on our health. Viruses are highly intelligent life forms that seem to know when it is time to attack. They silently lie in wait until the bacterial "pawns" weaken our army of immune antigens. Once the "kamikaze" bacterial invaders have risked their numbers in the service of weakening our defenses, potentially dangerous, indigenous viruses will then increase their numbers as they advance their attack on our immune system. First we upset intestinal pH with diet, stress, etc., and this acts as a precursor to bacterial and viral assaults. Systemic immune breakdown of this nature is the ultimate result of disregard for the Wu Wei. This, the Wu Way suggests, is why we have seen such a recent increase in chronic fatigue viruses or "yuppie flus" and mononucleosis, as well as ARC and AIDS conditions. After all, it is the current yuppie generation that grew up in the 50s and 60s. It was during the 50s and 60s that television helped to sell this generation sugared cereals, soft drinks, candies, cakes, pies, cookies, etc. Today, yuppies represent the generation that gave birth to "junk food." Not so coincidentally, it was during that same period of time America turned over her immune dependence to the use of broad-spectrum antibiotics.

Also of great importance, the Wu Way reminds us that our digestive immunity is under great duress as the result of excessive food variety. Because of the specific enzyme chains required to break down each food, the greater the food variety, the more complex the digestive work load; the more complex the digestive work load, the greater the probability for incomplete digestion, which may result in greater amounts of stored undigested food particles in the intestines, increasing the invasive bacterial populations there. We needn't get too complicated about all this. All we need do is follow the advice of the Wu Way and tune into our common sense and sensitivity as we endeavor to return to a more natural path. As nature continuously reminds us, the body machine performs best when it is worked least. Nature is synonymous with simplicity. Keep food selection simple. Keep food combinations to a minimum per meal, and keep in mind that your body was weaned on a history where there were no supermarkets and no planes or trains to transport foods transcontinentally. Digestion was simple, as it was intended by nature. Modern technology has opened the door to expansive dietary habits which have clearly taken their toll on human immunity.

Immunity as Part of the Whole

We can see the implication that our "highly evolved" ways have led us to yet another dead-end, with the laws of nature demanding that we glance once more at the road map to remind us how far we've strayed. The disease matrix goes far beyond a single-cell fungus, bacteria, or virus.

There is a natural "way of life" that, while appearing elusive to the analytical mind, remains very clear to our natural innate mind and body. When this process is accepted and cooperated with, the probability for unnatural disease and DIS-EASE decreases. Increased nutritional and immune awareness represent affirmative choice options designed to help realign one with his natural needs, and thus prevent the discordant system of disease. Being "turned on" from within, we become ever more "tuned in" to how foods affect us. We become a more complete "whole being," self-empowered with body, mind, spirit. This sensitivity and awareness will serve to remind us of our natural nutritional responsibilities so that we may pay closer attention to issues such as the highly dangerous bacteria and viruses in the body that, with certain foods, multiply and thus jeopardize our immune wellness.

We have all the power necessary to heal ourself. The healer lies within in the form of a healthy immune system that is wholistically supported in body, mind, and spirit. We must first abolish the desensitization and denial which remain at the core of our socio-cultural attitudes, erasing the adopted mindset of separatism from nature. It is unfortunate that we lack the understanding that everything is symbolically interconnected, bearing an endless network of systemic causes to an endless network of systemic effects. We must ultimately arrive at this spiritual understanding in order to construct a healthier, more wholistic lifestyle. If our fear of disease is any indication of our desire for wellness, then let it be noted that wellness can only be attained by first acknowledging the truth that we have perpetuated the very disease we fear by choosing to reject the nature to which we are infinitely tied.

In spite of our ego-driven gravitation toward self-gratification and denial, we must at last acknowledge the subtle, yet profound, dictates of universal law which remain in slumber deep within our psyches. Sometimes quite obviously, sometimes quite evasively, our conscience serves to remind us of the reality of the "whole" of life. These are laws that cannot be studied in textbook format. They must be summoned from deep within our natural conscience and common sense. In the end, we must realize that choosing to comply with nature ensures that true wellness will become reality. The long-term effects posed by the prospect of this "personal revolution" will surely prove transformative for a world of ailing bodies.

Poisonous Foods, Additives, and Lost Immunity

No single aspect of life affects the body's immune response more dramatically than nutrition. The unnatural feeding of the human body has led to a toxic overload of exceeding proportions. French surgeon and biologist Dr. Alexis Carrel (1873-

1944), recipient of the Nobel Prize for physiology and medicine, was a firm believer that nutrition was taking its toll on our natural body systems. He once said, "To a piece of living tissue in a test tube, we have to add an amount of fluid which is two thousand times its volume in order to prevent its being poisoned in a few days in its own wastes. If the tissue of the human body were de-toxified in a similar manner it would require about fifty thousand gallons of fluids to do the work."[9] The plain truth is, our food is hazardous to our health!

Overconsumption of fatty foods, fried foods, cured, processed, and injected red meats, refined sugars, and food additives are among the chief culprits in the area of diet-related immuno-suppression. Fried fatty foods result in deposits of chemical by-products called "free radicals." These free radicals are molecular fragments capable of severely damaging immune cells, which cause severe genetic damage and, in some cases, precede the onset of cancer. Such highly cured and processed meats as bacon, ham, bologna, salami, and hot dogs often contain sodium nitrate and sodium nitrite, additives designed to inhibit botulism and aflatoxin mold. When these nitrates and nitrites combine with various chemicals called amines, found in many proteins and other organic molecules, the end result is the formation of nitrosamines. Nitrosamines are widely accepted as the highest carcinogenic (cancer-causing) chemicals found in our foods. Nitrosamines can be produced with the combination of cured nitrate and nitrite meats and certain carbonated beverages, the classic example being the combination of beer or soft drink with a hot dog.

There is now strong evidence suggesting that diets high in fat increase the risk of colon and rectal cancers (the most frequent fatal forms of cancer), as well as leukemia and cancers of the breast, pancreas, gall bladder, ovary, uterus, and prostate. Many researchers believe that elevated bile acids in the colon

---

[9] Kurt W. Donsbach, D.C., N.D., *Preventive Organic Medicine,* (New Caanan, CT: Keats Publishing, 1976), p. 50.

break down into lithocholic and deoxycholic acids, both very dangerous carcinogens.

At this point we need to take a closer look at the two major classifications of dietary fats—saturated and unsaturated. Saturated fats are fatty acids whose carbon bonds are all attached to hydrogen atoms and are generally considered a more "solid" fat, such as the fats in animal products. Unsaturated fats, often referred to as either poly- or mono-unsaturates, have some of their carbon bonds free and unattached to hydrogen atoms, and are therefore less "solid" or more fragmented, such as the fats in most fish and vegetable products. It is generally accepted that we are far better off nutritionally to avoid an excess of saturated fats, and opt instead for either the poly- or mono-unsaturated fats. Many people have been instructed to guard against heart disease by keeping a vigilant watch on cholesterol and saturated fat levels, replacing butter with margarine, lard with polyunsaturated oils.

We are now beginning to see that there are other previously unsuspected immuno-suppressive considerations with regard to the excessive use of polyunsaturated fats. Though these polyunsaturated fats, predominantly obtained from vegetable oils, have been shown to increase immune antibody responsiveness, an excess of these fats in laboratory animals has been shown to produce profound immuno-suppression in the thymus gland (immune headquarters). Immune protective white blood cells, or "T-cells," make up more than half the lymphocyte population and are manufactured and incubated in the thymus gland, located beneath the breastbone. These T-cells are often referred to as identification cells because their specialty is to identify and destroy the invader (bacteria, virus, etc.) or send orders to B-cell antibodies (another group of specialized attack cells) to carry out the mission—a kind of search and destroy tactic. The key here is that polyunsaturates undergo a process of lipid peroxidation in the body. The more unsaturated the fat, the less density; the less density, the less insulation or protection the fat has from exposure to heat. As we've pointed out, it has been widely documented that free radical peroxide chemical chains, which are the end result of fried (overheated) uninsulated fats, are cancer-causing. Moreover, the heat of the human body (98.6°F) will create the same conditions as this prolonged overexposure to heat from cooking.

Many scientists now believe that the increased cancer rates of the past twenty years come as a result of the great American campaign to reduce the risk of heart disease. To lessen the risk of heart disease we were told to eat fats that were less saturated and less solid, that do not contribute to clogged arteries. Now we are finding that these "thinner" fats are less protected from heat, which, in turn, create dangerous free radical peroxide carcinogens in the body, increasing immuno-suppression and the risk of cancer. In response to this dilemma, many doctors and nutritionists are now recommending canola oils, olive oils and peanut oils, which are referred to as mono-unsaturates and are more protected from oxidation. The typical vegetable oil is about 80% saturated, where as olive and peanut oils are about 50% polyunsaturated, and therefore, provide nutritional support in the prevention of heart disease and carcinogenic immune depletion. Along with the immune-depleting elements of saturated fats and carcinogens in most processed meats, we must also consider the immunological ill effects of hormones, antibiotics, pesticides, and chemical additives. Beyond these fats, our drug and chemically indoctrinated culture has amassed an array of poisons that have found their way into our foods. Food additives, insecticides, and toxic hormones are among such poisons.

DES (diethylstilbesterol) is one of the most common hormones injected into cattle and poultry for quick growth and artificial fatty weight gain prior to slaughter. This hormone, banned in most European countries and Canada, has been shown to cause cancerous tumors and interfere with pituitary growth hormone function in animals. Many of these other countries actually refuse to import American beef because of DES's suspected ill-effects on the human immune system. DES is a growth-stimulating hormone that works by slowing down the metabolism. As the metabolism slows down, fat cells are able to generate at a much faster rate. DES really came to the public's attention when it was administered to millions of pregnant American women during the 1950s and 60s to prevent miscarriage. In the late 60s and early 70s, medical research showed that it was not only ineffective but dangerous, because it greatly increased the risk of cancer among its users and their offspring. Soon thereafter DES was banned in food processing but such high volumes were used in livestock and poultry for so long that residues are still found today. Antibiotics are also used in raising livestock and poultry. A vast number of cattle and poultry are fed 30 to 40 pounds of grain per day, with a transformed yield of only three to four pounds of muscle and fat. There is constant overfeeding for quick high-volume growth. This overfeeding often causes liver abscesses and bacterial infections that seriously affect profit margins, so the livestock are often fed the antibiotic oxytetracycline.

When animals are kept in overcrowded quarters, engulfed in a bag of their own excrement and fed around the clock beneath fluorescent lamps, they are highly susceptible to disease. Hence, they are usually given large doses of strepto-mycin, another antibiotic, as well as tranquilizers for sickness and discomfort. It is becoming difficult to determine which is more of a threat to us, the dangerous bacteria carried by our livestock or the equally dangerous antibiotic residues given to control bacterial proliferation. Both represent potential health problems to the consumer.

Each year more than 2,700 chemicals are administered to more than 20 million animals used for human consumption. More than 270,000 cases of food poisoning result in approximately 300 deaths. Some theorists now believe that the recent sudden decline in human immune response (evidenced in the increase in AIDS and many cancers) is, in part, the result of the consumption of hidden antibiotic residues in milk, beef, and poultry. On a long-term basis, the standing presence of antibiotics in the intestinal tract could destroy populations of protective microfloral bacteria, thus beginning a downward immune spiral, opening the door to further bacterial and viral susceptibility.

Another area of increasing concern is pesticides. They minimize crop damage by killing insects and fungi in commercial food crops designed to feed live stock, but then find their way into our beef and poultry products. Questions of concern include specific selection and proper dosage and timing of pesticide usage, which are ultimately important to human health.

DDT and Endrin are two of the more widely used organic, synthetic insecticides of the chlorinated hydrocarbon (or organochlorine) chains most feared by ecologists and conservationists. They are most feared because they possess an uncommon chemical stability. "They do not break down in the environment but tend to be recycled through food chains; being fat-soluble, they accumulate in high concentrations in the tissues of animals which are at the top of the food chain. Despite intensive study no one even today is quite sure how the chlorinated hydrocarbons kill, but they are known to affect the central nervous system."[10] Some other members of this group include aldrin, chlordane, heptachlor, and toxaphene. In addition, other popular groups include extremely toxic organic phosphates such as malathion and parathion.

Laboratory tests have shown that high concentrations of these organic pesticides cause serious illness and death for many plants and animals. Many of the pesticides still used today are closely related to "nerve gases"; they are designed to kill pests by paralyzing their central nervous systems. Under great

---

[10] Frank Graham Jr., *Since Silent Spring*, (New York: Fawcett Crest Books, Houghton Mifflin, 1970), p. 30.

pressure from mounting public concern, the Food and Drug Administration (FDA) limited their general use in 1965 from 0.25 part per million to 0.1 part per million. Both the FDA and many other federal and state departments constantly conduct research aimed at further documenting the ill effects on humans, with the intention of developing less toxic chemicals.

With all this research and testing, the FDA and the Environmental Protection Agency (EPA) still claim they do not really know the full extent of the danger posed to humans by many of these insecticides. Yet, nearly 50,000 pesticide products in 600 chemical categories are currently in full-scale use today. It takes years of study to evaluate the long-term effects of a single pesticide on a single test animal. To date the EPA has developed data on only 192 chemicals, and has fully reviewed and registered only two of them with the FDA.

"It is probable that continued exposure to low levels of toxic agents will eventually result in a great variety of delayed pathological manifestations creating physiological misery and increasing the medical load," one distinguished physician writes. "The point of importance here is that the worst pathological effects of environmental pollutants will not be detected at the time of exposure; indeed they may not become evident until several decades later."[11] Do we have the time to wait for science and politics? The limitations and politics of science and logic alone pose a great threat to our survival. If man is truly to become healed through whole-ism then he must acknowledge and put to work his own inner common sense and sensitivity. To quote Henry Beston, author of *The Freeman,* "Some spiritual instinct has shaken itself free and has refused to take the scientific vision of nature as complete...."[12]

The Wu Way reminds us that there are alternatives to pesticides. Many non-toxic, organic agents may be used which pose no harm to life and, therefore, our food support system.

---

[11] ibid., p. 139.

[12] ibid., p. 20.

Unfortunately, there is little or no profit motivation in pursuing the use of such agents. All the reader need do for edification is consult organic gardening literature available in most libraries. (See comprehensive list in National Groups with Regional and Local Affiliates).

A 1989 *Newsweek* article reported: "A recent controversial report by the environmental group Natural Resources Defense Council (NRDC) concluded that some three million children are exposed to neurotoxic pesticides above what the EPA considers an 'acceptable' level. Because children eat relatively more fruits and vegetables than adults, they receive several times the exposure to carcinogenic pesticides than their parents. As a result, says the NRDC, 5,500 to 6,200 of today's preschoolers may eventually have cancer because of childhood exposure to just eight of these pesticides."[13]

It has been well documented that pesticides pose a great threat to the human nervous, respiratory, and immune systems, especially since the publication of Rachel Carson's *Silent Spring* in 1962. Her work was a pioneering exposé of the risks of both long-term and concentrated exposure to pesticides. Even protection from these risks poses a precarious dilemma, for organically grown produce, though not sprayed with pesticides, can contain poisonous residues. "In one test, the New York State Department of Agriculture and Markets found pesticide residues on 30% of a sampling of organic foods bought in health food stores, compared to only 20% found in most common chain stores."[14] This condition has nothing to do with fraud, but rather with the saturation of pesticides in the soil, in environmental moisture, and even rain. It is currently next to impossible to grow food free of pesticides because of the previous 50 years of industrialized farming in our highly technological, overpopulated, profit-pressured world.

---

[13] *Newsweek,* March 27, 1989, p. 20.

[14] *Wholesome Diet,* (Alexandria, VA: Time Life Books, 1981).

Sugar Bare (The Stripped Carbohydrate)

The average American now consumes 130 pounds of sugar per year. Sucrose or sugar is a carbohydrate refined eighty times from its natural state, stripped of 90 percent of its bulk as well as *all* of its vitamins and minerals. To absorb this "predigested" product, the body must deplete many of its existing vitamin and mineral reserves, leaving it in a state of biological stress and immune susceptibility. Included among the depleted elements are antioxidants such as zinc, selenium, and vitamin B-1, whose absence leaves the body with marked immune susceptibility.

One of the best-known immune precursor antioxidants is the mineral zinc. Zinc is an extremely important immune system stimulant capable of promoting immune support T-cell populations and B-cell populations, as well as protective bacterial activity and antibody production. In order for this immune "superstar" to be assimilated in the human body it must be introduced in proper ratio to the toxic mineral cadmium. The ideal ratio is 40:1 zinc to cadmium; in most unrefined carbohydrates (for example, whole grain products), the ratio is generally 100:1. On the other hand, *refined* carbohydrates present a serious ratio debit, because much of the zinc is processed out, leaving high amounts of cadmium. White flour products, white rice, etc., carry a 10:1 ratio, hardly enough to support zinc's requirements. Sugar is worse yet, with a reverse ratio of 100:1 cadmium to zinc.

In terms of immuno-digestive mechanics, the pancreas, in order to metabolize large amounts of simple sugars, is called upon to release large amounts of insulin to transport the converted energy created by these sugars (80 percent of which goes to the brain) throughout the body. This excess insulin triggering has been linked not only to atherosclerosis, increased fats in the blood stream, and low blood sugar, but immuno-suppressive inhibition of pituitary growth hormone. This is especially significant before bedtime, as most of our immune precursor growth hormone is secreted during the first two hours of sleep.

Growth hormone is a polypeptide hormone secreted by the anterior lobe of the pituitary gland in the brain and is vital in terms of immune cell repair. As immune cells are often damaged by the many viruses and bacteria in the system, growth hormones are released to seek out the damaged cells and repair them where possible. Sugar not only impairs this process, but actually helps to create a state in the intestines suited to development of harmful and invasive bacteria capable of damaging our immune cells, thus serving to "aid and abet the enemy."

This negative bacterial influence sucrose (sugar) imposes on the body is a most important immune consideration. The lower intestines store 98 percent of the body's anaerobic bacteria. These indigenous bacteria carry both good and bad influence. Some of the good bacteria are of a protective microfloral variety, acting as members of our respective immune armies, whose function is to destroy harmful pathogenic bacteria. At the same time, there remain complexes of harmful, potentially invasive bacteria which may produce toxins in the intestines with the ability to cause extensive immunological damage.

The key to prevention here is to keep the harmful populations down and the protective populations up. Sugar (sucrose) is at the top of the list of foods that promote development of harmful bacterial populations. The mechanism is largely a matter of pH, or acidity vs. alkalinity. For the body to maintain a protective bacterial edge, we need to consume four parts alkaline to one part acid-forming foods. Sugar and very refined carbohydrates contribute to a general acid condition in the body, especially when accompanied by a lack of vegetables and unrefined alkaline grains in the diet. This situation, in turn, promotes the acid intestinal pH preferred by most pathogenic, immune-depleting bacteria.

Excessive consumption of processed sugar is profoundly implicated in a number of human health concerns including osteoporosis, heart disease, and behavioral problems. According to a 1975 study published by the *Journal of Laboratory and Cinical Medicine*, "Evidence that Glucose Ingestion Inhibits Net Renal Tubular Reabsorption of Calcium and Magnesium in Man."... "A high sugar diet plays a significant role in calcium loss and softening of the bones."[15]

Sheldon Reiser, Ph.D., and a team of researchers at the USDA's Carbohydrate Nutrition Laboratory in Beltsville, Maryland recently performed an extensive twelve-week blood sugar/blood fat study, clearly establishing that both insulin and triglyceride levels have a tendency to rise simultaneously. In lay terms, Dr. Reiser's team substantiated a direct link between excessive consumption of processed sugar and the development of coronary artery disease.[16] Alex Schauss, a state corrections officer for the Washington State Criminal Justice Training Commission, has become nationally renowned for his "Body Chemistry and Offender Behavior," program which strongly points out that repeat offender criminal behavior is directly linked to psychological sickness which is directly influenced by excessive refined sugar consumption. Schauss reports that most of their repeat offenders consume from 300 to 600 pounds of sugar per year, about two to four times the national average, and that consequently 90 percent of their inmate population have metabolic blood sugar disorders. According to Schauss, many of the symptoms they've observed, directly associated with excessive sugar consumption, include irritability, paranoia, sudden violent behavior, and general criminal behavior.

---

[15] J. Leman, *Journal of Laboratory and Clinical Medicine,* "Evidence that Glucose Ingestion Inhibits Net Renal Tubular Reabsorption of Calcium and Magnesium in Man" et. al., no. 4, 1970, pp. 578-585.

[16] *Prevention's New Encylcopedia of Common Diseases,* (Emmaus, PA: Rodale Press, 1984), pp. 493-495.

"Excessive" appears to be the operative word here, but just how much is too much? Many food scientists and nutritionists now tell us that the liver, which metabolizes sugars through a process called anaerobic glycolosis, can only break down 50 grams at a time. The excess then, if not burned quickly, clearly stresses the liver as it must be converted into saturated fat for storage. Here some clearer pictures of just how easy it is to exceed the 50 gram criteria. Based on 100 grams=20 tea-spoons=3 1/2 ounces=400 calories: one candy bar=60 grams, 1 slice of chocolate caker=100 grams, 6 ounces of soft drink=180 grams, 1/2 cup of unsweetened fruit juice=100 grams.[17]

Perhaps all we really need to do is remind ourselves that refined sugar was not provided by nature and not available for the preceding million years of human evolution.

Other Food-Related Drugs

Coffee

The use of caffeine and alcohol is also directly related to the human body immune de-evolution syndrome. Dr. John Milton, Professor of Surgery at Ohio State University and specialist in oncology, has found that excessive intake of methylxanthines (active chemicals in caffeine) can cause benign breast disease and prostate problems. Dr. Phillip Cole reported that a strong relationship exists between coffee consumption and cancer of the bladder and urinary tract.[18] New evidence continues to mount implicating foodstuffs like caffeine, theophylline, and theobromine (methylxanthines found in coffee, tea, chocolate and colas) in fibrocystic breast disease. Caffeine has the potential for such high toxicity in the system that lethal doses have actually been estimated at around 10 g. One mug (10-12

---

[17] ibid., p. 212.

[18] Earl Mindell, *Earl Mindell's Vitamin Bible,* (New York: Warner Books, 1979), p. 256.

ounce) of drip percolated coffee gives you approximately 300 mg. With three mugs equaling approximately one gram, the lethal dose is approached at approximately 30 mugs of coffee per day. Perhaps this sounds a bit sensationalized, yet I distinctly remember one client, a construction worker, relating to me in his diet history that he consumed nearly 50 cups or approximately 25 mugs per day without even realizing it. Coffee/caffeine have become so much a part of our culture and lifestyle that we consume it without regard.

But caffeine appears not to be the only culprit labeled in the apparent coffee-cancer risk analogy. Decaffeinated coffee continues to show the same risks. "When coffee was first decaffeinated, trichloroethylene was used as a caffeine bleaching agent. This carbon-to-chlorine chemical bond proved to be equally carcinogenic to coffee drinkers. Methylene chloride was then substituted for trichloroethylene. Though it appears to be safer in early reports it, too, introduces the same carbon-to-chlorine bond as does trichloroethylene and a number of toxic and carcinogenic insecticides."

Not unlike sugar (sucrose), coffee, whether caffeinated or decaffeinated, is a highly acidic substance that affects the body's lower intestinal pH. Keeping in mind that it is of the utmost importance to maintain a 4:1 alkaline-to-acid pH for general and immunological wellness, coffee, with its high acidity, imposes an acid pH on the body. Consumed in high volumes over extended periods, it may carry an immune risk factor. "Coffee and tea both contain tannic acid. And researchers from India recently found that when they fed a diet rich in tannic acid to laboratory rats, the rats experienced damage to their heart muscles, and an increase in the cholesterol levels of their blood. The rats received the human equivalent of six cups or more of black tea or black coffee per day."[19]

---

[19] *Indian Journal of Nutrition and Dietetics,* vol. 16, no. 9, 1979.

Alcohol

Alcohol is the most widely used drug in the history of the planet. Excessive alcohol intake leads to blood abnormalities, degeneration of the heart muscle, peripheral neuropathy, muscle disorders, degeneration of the central nervous system, chronic lung disease, malignancies of the head and neck, intestinal malabsorption, low blood sugar levels, liver disease, and increased susceptibility to infection. It is specifically this area of malabsorption that has been shown to increase susceptibility to infection which in turn implicates alcohol in immune dysfunction.

Alcohol interferes with the body's assimilation of all the B and C vitamins and many trace minerals, including zinc, potassium, and magnesium, to mention a few. All of these nutrients play a vital role in the production and maintenance of immune antibodies which are all impaired by alcohol intake. In fact, the immune implications of alcohol usage are extensive.

All healthy mammals, including people, make a small amount of alcohol in their bodies as part of normal metabolism. The average person makes about one ounce of alcohol every day by normal metabolism. In order to metabolize this internally created alcohol, man and the other mammals have special enzymes, particularly in their livers. These enzymes handle both the internally made alcohol and also alcohol drunk in beverages. In the first step, the enzyme called alcohol dehydrogenase converts alcohol to acetaldehyde, a chemical which can damage the body in several ways. It can create abnormal chemical bonds in important large molecules like proteins (resulting in skin wrinkling and artery hardening and loss of elasticity) and damage DNA (resulting in abnormal cell function, birth defects, and even cancer). This abnormal chemical bonding process is called crosslinking and is the same process that causes your car's rubber windshield wipers to harden and become brittle and that converts (tans) soft, moist cattle skin into hard, dry, stiff leather. It is also the same process used to embalm cadavers, which employs close chemical relatives of acetaldehyde such as formaldehyde and glutaraldehyde. When cross-linking takes place in the lungs, we call the result emphysema. Another way acetaldehyde causes damage is when it is nonenzymatically oxidized in the body, creating dangerous and reactive chemical fragments called free radicals. These free radicals can cause cancer, birth defects, cross-linking, atherosclerosis, and are implicated as major causative factors in aging.[20]

Normal people who are not obsessive alcohol users have no trouble with this alcohol conversion process. However, if we drink alcohol fast enough, the acetaldehyde can accumulate faster than our body's ability to eliminate it. Acetaldehyde and its free radical potential represents the most dangerous immune threat from alcohol usage. It is the acetaldehyde, in fact, that precipitates the marked increase in risk that drinkers have of developing cancer, atherosclerosis, cataracts, brain damage, premature skin aging, and general decreasing resistance to disease.

Nutrient destruction and immune interference have even been questioned with regard to those who are not considered long-term heavy drinkers. A researcher at Ohio State University reports that six or seven drinks a day for as little as two weeks can throw the digestive system into reverse, causing the small intestine to begin secreting fluids that flush food from the body before it is used.[21] Once these digestive secretions (and thus the nutrients they are designed to help us assimilate) are interfered with, the all-important maintenance functions of the body become neglected. The liver, responsible for more than

---

[20] Durk Pearson & Sandy Shaw, *Life Extension,* (New York: Warner Book, 1981), pp. 269-270.

[21] *Prevention's New Encyclopedia of Common Diseases,* p. 941.

a third of the body's digestive metabolism, as well as immune support, becomes overworked and eventually debilitated.

Alcoholism is currently ranked as America's fourth worst health care problem, and the number one cause of death in the 35 to 65 age group. Alcohol use and the current widespread use of drugs in general might be viewed more importantly as effects or results of our compulsive, de-evolving way of life.

Intolerances (Allergies) and Immune De-Evolution

In recent years there has been a great deal of conjecture about food allergies. As many as thirty million Americans may suffer from either genetic food intolerance or food allergies of some kind. Allergic reactions are varied: digestive pains, hives, headaches, asthma, bronchial congestion, muscle and joint aches, nausea, even irrational, "neurotic" emotional and mental behavior. Among the most common offenders are: milk and dairy products, wheat, corn, shellfish, citrus, legumes (including all peas, beans, soy products, and nuts), eggs, and "nightshade" vegetables or fruits such as tomatoes, eggplant, peppers, and cabbages.

An allergic reaction has a specific definition: when exposed to the suspected food, the person's body produces immune antibodies resulting in symptoms. Current medical practice requires skin tests (RAS) where the skin is scratched and exposed to food extracts to observe antibody reactions, as well as blood tests where blood platelets are exposed to food extracts so that they will display either positive or negative aggregation response, in order to confirm diagnosis.

There are many current health care practitioners who feel that the food allergy question, while being one of the most misunderstood, undiagnosed issues, is one of the truly important links in the human de-evolution crisis. As the mind and spirit are continually bombarded with the stressful task of adapting to modern life, there is a breakdown in body functions such as digestion. Stress often predetermines digestive efficiency and thus food tolerance. As this breakdown reaches other body systems, triggering symptoms in acute and chronic proportions, general tolerance to any stress, whether physical, mental, or emotional, lessens, creating a pattern of disharmony. It goes from emotional to physical and back again, setting up a repercussive systemic illness response.

Growing ever more popular among many whole-istic health practitioners is the belief that blood and skin alone are not enough in determining food allergies. For many years cytoxic lab allergy specialists told us that exposures to food allergens brought about an array of unpredictable reactions. This implies that proper diagnosis is more of an art than a science in light of the complicated variables the human condition often presents. It was often noted that "no two people would react the same to any one allergen." For example, one person exposed to a dairy product might exhibit migraine headaches, while another would exhibit bronchial congestion. Furthermore, a person might be exposed to a food or food extract on one day and show no significant reaction, while a significant reaction could occur as many as ten days later. Some theorists believe this signifies that an individual could consume a food on a given day, appear fine, and then have an allergic reaction up to ten days later, due to severely impaired digestion/assimilation. To further complicate matters, the symptoms might be as elusive as a slight passing depression or mental "fog."

In answer to these questions, an array of recent self-help diet books are intent on instructing their readers with both the merits and the mechanics of "rotation diets," which are designed to allow the digestive tract time to clear itself of food overload by eating each food on a rotation basis. Example: If I were to eat apples on Monday then I would abstain from apples for the ensuing three days and eat apples again on Friday. This type of diet would be set up so that all foods were used in a similar way for an extended period of time. Of course, there are many variations on this theme, with each advocate adding a personal theory and thus a change here and there, but the basis for rotation is to simplify the digestive workload.

Just as with blood and skin tests, the flaw in rotation diets is that they are either too general or lacking in boldness and creativity—important ingredients in any healing art. They fail to address subtler, unseen human responses to potential allergens. The subtler the response detection, the earlier the intervention, the more effective the prevention. These subtleties, so easily accessed via the skeletal muscular system's electrical neuro-transmission network, hold many secrets about the often over-looked nuances of our level of wellness. There are various forms of kinesiology (non-invasive muscle testing) that enable us to determine food and other insensitivities (intolerances) that not only take human emotion and spirit into consideration, but actually rely on them for vital healing information. (The topic of kinesiology and human force fields will be more fully discussed in Chapter 3)

Whether inclined to blood or skin tests, rotation diets, or kinesiology testing, one thing remains perfectly clear: any foods taken into the body ultimately contribute to either wellness or disease. Any foods that are poorly digested prompt the triggering of antibody secretions to neutralize their toxic presence, thus placing a great deal of stress and burden on body immunity. When the body's immune system is already constantly busy about the work of neutralizing the presence of viruses (with more than 400 present at all times), bacteria, environmental pollutants, etc., the last thing it needs is the added task of filtering and immunologically neutralizing the presence of unwelcome food toxins. As we can see, these toxins are not exclusively provoked by "junk foods," but from undigested foods that might initially appear harmless and even healthful. Although this is a much-debated issue, common sense reminds us that the human body was weaned on organic, unprocessed, indigenous, seasonally-rotated foods since the dawn of evolution.

For a million years our food selection was naturally prede-termined. There was no refrigeration, no industrial processing or preserving. Throughout history, most of our ancestors were raised on the foods grown and harvested right on their own land. Wholesome grains, fruits, and vegetables were indig-enous and seasonal with limited addition of fish, meat, and dairy products. Only a select few enjoyed rare, imported goods. Not all land was suitable for grazing and therefore not all people had access to beef and dairy products. Most of our ancestors were non-migrational, at least for extended periods of time, and even those who were, were generally restricted by distance, especially by today's standards. For the most part, inhabitants of the tropics ate the yield of their tropical habitat while inhabitants of the more temperate zones would have little or no exposure to tropical foods, and vice versa. They, too, would be restricted by the dictates of time, space, and technology.

Nowadays, we are far less restricted by the limitations previously imposed by nature. We have the means and ingenuity to fly foods around the world each day, importing and exporting wherever the supply can meet the demand. Throughout the million years of human history, the average human ate from a variety of no more than six or seven foods at best, and therefore limitations imposed by the seasons, climate, soil, and weather, ensured that no one's digestive system ever became too overworked. Over the generations, our digestive systems have been genetically and indigenously adapted far more profoundly then we might believe. In fact, each of our bodies with its unique, specific complement of digestive enzymes, is genetically imprinted so that it can most efficiently digest only those indigenous foods to which for generations its lineage was most commonly exposed. Con-versely, if for twenty-five of the past thirty generations a family lineage was not exposed to dairy products, and hence lacked genetically adapted, specialized enzymes to digest milk, we might assume a strong probability for milk intolerances (allergies). Dr. Hal Huggins, D.D.S., in his article, "The Significance of Mutation in Preventive Dentistry," speaks of " . . . an ancestral diet concept, which is based upon the hypothesis that a specie lives and eats the foods in one area for 1,000 years or more, and becomes adapted to the foods in that area. If a specie moves to a new habitat, it comes in contact with new foods that require different intestinal bacteria to digest them, and modifications must be made. The specie may need another 1,000 years to adapt to the new diet."[22]

Digestion is highly specialized, making the likelihood of food intolerances strong wherever there exists an overexpanded variety, abundance, and/or volume of food. Just think, there are seventy-five trillion cells in our bodies with more than one thousand enzymes (many of which are digestive) at work in each cell. Most enzymes participate in only one chemical reaction on a single substance, although some do act on compounds. There are, on average, over eighty thousand digestive enzymes in the body, some specifically for protein digestion (proteases), some for fat digestion (lipases), and some for carbohydrate digestion (amylases). A single cell contains thousands of enzymes for thousands of different specialized actions. At the same time, each different food requires separate enzymes and enzyme compounds to perform various functions in the digestive process. Each food has a different pH factor which dictates the efficiency with which each enzyme performs its work, as each enzyme performs optimally at a specific pH.

In a much simpler sense, the less work required of our digestive systems, the more efficient the digestion. The more overworked a digestive system, as is often the case today, the more non-digestive toxic residues build up in the body, requiring immune antibodies to neutralize their subsequent

---

[22] *Let's Live,* March 1989, p. 68.

pathogenic presence. As long as allergens are being ingested, the immune system must continually react to them. With this continual preoccupation with food-related toxins, the immune defense system becomes distracted from its other important functions such as protection from invasive bacteria and viruses, as well as immune antibody repair. Accumulated food allergens also form degenerative concentrations of protein putrefaction and starch fermentation in the colon; both interfere with our protective microfloral (bacterial) synthesis. The predominant bacteria in the colon, *Escherichia coli* or *E. coli*, are employed to release such gases as methane, carbon dioxide, hydrogen, lactic and acetic acid, as well as such toxic gases as indol and phenol. These protective *E. coli* bacteria are also responsible for the microbial synthesis of the vitamins and minerals responsible for our body's daily maintenance functions. These toxic accumulations in the colon, largely the result of improper food assimilation from unidentified food intolerances or allergens, have also been directly linked to colon-rectal and other cancers.

The human digestive system, which depended for a million years on complex, fibrous, simplified diets from a limited variety of foods, is now overworked, undernourished, toxic, and therefore directly implicated in disease and immune de-evolution.

Our choice to willfully divorce ourselves from nature is painfully evident in the area of nutrition. Our foods bring great sensate pleasure, even as they disregard our body's natural needs. Disregarding our body's natural needs only ensures the de-evolutionary spiral of unnatural disease. This madness will not end as long as we victimize yet one more future generation with highly-processed, denatured food.

Insuring a Future for De-Evolution

In January 1977, the Senate issued a report of the Select Committee on Nutrition and Hunger Needs, chaired by Senator

George McGovern. In his opening statements Senator McGovern concluded:

During this century, the composition of the average diet in the United States has changed radically. Complex carbohydrates—fruit, vegetables, and grain products—which were the mainstay of the diet, now play a minority role. At the same time, fat and sugar consumption have risen to the point where these two dietary elements alone now comprise at least 60% of the total caloric intake.

In the view of doctors and nutritionists consulted by the Select Committee, these and other changes in the diet amount to a wave of malnutrition—of both over- and under-consumption that may be as profoundly damaging to the nation's health as the widespread contagious diseases of the early part of the century.

The over-consumption of fat, generally, and saturated fat in particular, as well as cholesterol, sugar, salt, and alcohol have been related to six of the ten leading causes of death: heart disease, cancer, cerebrovascular disease, diabetes, arteriosclerosis, and cirrhosis of the liver.

Malnutrition is the single most common cause of general immune deficiency and sickness among humans. Cell-mediated immunity is severely impaired, and thymus and lymph tissues are prone to early and severe atrophy. The same serum antibodies secreted by the body for the neutralization of food allergens are actually higher during long periods of malnutrition—specifically protein-energy malnutrition, which afflicts one hundred million children under the age of five. Though this malnutrition is most common in third-world countries, it is also on the increase in America's inner city ghettos,[23] and incidently affects 15 percent of patients in acute care hospitals in this country. At any rate, it is most important that we know that malnutrition is right here in our own back yard. In essence, the depletion of our immune systems begins with the growing

---

[23] Werner, *Maximum Immunity,* p. 97.

malnutrition to which Senator McGovern alluded during the Senate subcommittee hearings on Nutrition and Human Needs. Malnutrition is in our hospitals, in our work place, in our restaurants, in our markets, and, worse, in our children's schools. The neglected diets of our children will continue to give rise to endless future generations of immune depletion. If current trends are allowed to continue, the unnatural feeding of our youth and their resultant systemic patterns of disease will surely continue to jeopardize the future of disease prevention. This unfortunate tragedy will ultimately be the result of our growing commitment to profit without principle— profit that will prove most unaffordable.

As recently as fifteen years ago the American Cancer Society established that obese people were 50 percent more likely to suffer from cancers of the uterus, gall bladder, stomach, colon, and breast, yet in those same fifteen years the incidence of obesity increased by 40 percent in America's high school and grade school children.

A recent medical research study in Baltimore County, Maryland established that 35 percent of America's school children have abnormally high cholesterol levels in excess of 175 mg per dosage liter. According to Dr. Gerald Baronsen, the Director of the famed Bogaloosa Heart Study in Bogaloosa, Louisiana, "Fifty percent of the nation will die of heart disease if the current diets of our school children remain unchanged."[24] With current health care costs for heart disease in excess of $50 billion per year, we can ill afford this preventable consequence. Dr. Peter Kwiterovitch, initiator of a Family Nutrition Education Program at Johns Hopkins Medical School and staunch nutrition advocate, stated, "Proper diet could cut heart disease in America by 50 percent."

Our children eat more than any children in the history of our planet, yet they suffer from malnutrition as the result of empty

---

[24] Dr. Gerald Baronsen, Bogaloosa Heart Study, New Orleans, LA: New Orleans Ashview Medical Center, (504) 568-4654.

calories from foods high in saturated fats, sugar, salt, and additives. The ensuing vitamin and mineral deficiencies manifest themselves in a host of physical and mental symptoms. Cancer, heart disease, depression, suicide, alcoholism, and drug addiction are becoming widespread problems among our youth, each with roots tied deeply to malnutrition.

In the 80s, breakfast became obsolete, lunch became fast food, and dinner became microwave frozen dinners. Dr. Stephanie Beling, well-known pediatric endocrinologist, agrees that there is a current wave of malnutrition among children, pointing to school lunch programs as a major contributor.

The National School Lunch Program began in 1946 for the stated purpose of insuring school children a wholesome school lunch. The program still feeds 27 million children annually but with very different implications. Today the program is a dumping ground for vast surpluses purchased from farms by the federal government and provided free to schools. These surplus commodities include high-fat whole milk, cheeses, and meat–often fat-fried. Low-fat alternatives which should be freely provided to our schools are only available at a cost which is not even a priority in the budgets of most school systems. The same can be said for children's exercise programs, another sad, de-evolving story. As many as 40 percent of our youth between the ages of six and seventeen cannot do a single pull-up, with only the State of Illinois maintaining former President Kennedy's physical fitness program in its school system. According to a 1986 Presidential Study on Children's Fitness and Health, school requirements for physical fitness have slowly made their way to the bottom of the priority list with an average of only sixty hours per year, compared with the twenty-five hours of television watched by the average school aged child *per week*. TV and its advertising are readily implicated in this malnutritive, physically unfit, de-evolutionary scenario of our youth.

By the age of eighteen the average child will have watched twenty thousand food commercials. According to a recent study reported in *Journal of Nutrition Education,* 80 percent of those twenty thousand commercials are for food products that by government standards are well below the norm in nutritional value. The emphasis is not on food quality or health or integrity, but on profit, greed, and deception. These commercials are hot, slick, convincing, and gimmicky, designed only to influence the buying power of our youth, with no genuine interest in their well-being. Teens and younger children currently draw allowances estimated at more than $6 billion per year. Another study indicates that 78 percent of all children influence what their parents buy at the store. Our youth have economic power along with innocence and vulnerability, a deadly combination ideal for manipulation by Madison Avenue.

Even if children are well-intentioned and getting honest accountable information, which is unlikely, they are still so brainwashed and overwhelmed, not to mention acculturated and even addicted to damaging denatured foods, that they really do not stand a chance. Clearly, the free enterprise system is sacrosanct in our society, but where do we draw the line between sentient and serpentine? Consider the advertising budgets submitted in 1988 for the food industries most likely to influence our children to purchase products that are below normal nutritional value (high in sodium, fat, and/or sugar):

Combined cereal companies:	$654 million
Combined soft drink companies:	$389 million
Combined gum and candy:	$405 million
Combined fast food industry:	$1 billion

With MacDonald's budget alone exceeding $366 million, an estimated 100 new cereals and 1,400 new snacks are introduced yearly, clear indications of the growth potential of the existing market. Children, and many of their families, receive little or no other information related to food and nutrition while being blitzed with billions of dollars worth of powerful, one-sided, often distorted ad campaigns. It is disheartening to learn that a mere 300 out of 17,000 high schools recently surveyed in this country offer courses in general nutrition. While it is true that doctors are starting to reconsider the role of nutrition education as important to their patients' needs, it is doubtful that children are going to find the information from them either. A recent study points to the disillusioning fact that only 25 percent of all American medical schools offer an elective course in basic nutrition. While children remain completely in the dark, profiteers of tasty, fashionable, and convenient sugar, fat, and sodium-laden foods continue to thrive on their ill-fated ignorance. In the past fifteen years pizza franchises have risen to 20,000, up 590 percent, and burger franchises to 35,000—nearly doubling. A new MacDonald's franchise opens up every seventeen hours.

All this growth and advertising is somewhat hard to swallow when we hear from a Senate subcommittee report that six of the ten leading causes of death in our country are related to diet. And it gets harder to swallow when we hear from noted and respected medical researchers that 50 percent of our current child population can be expected to die of diet-related heart disease, 100 percent of which is preventable. We spend so much of our time and resources on advertising, manufacturing, and marketing substandard and artificial foods to our children, and so little time on educating them about nutrition and feeding them properly. To have a truly productive society, our first priority must be in caring for our youth. It is most important that we know it is affordable, beyond a doubt, to ensure proper nutrition for our children. Feeding our children well is much less a matter of dollars, and much more a matter of proper education and commitment. While the fast food industry feeds our economic system, it preys upon our youth. The very systems we have created to improve our quality of life at last feed off of us. It is a Frankenstein scenario, where once resplendent expressions of our resilience and advancement as an enterprising society have become monsters of our own design. If our world is to be a better place, then it must be a healthier place. If our world is to be a healthier place, then surely it must begin with healthier humans. A generation of healthier humans begins with healthier children. Our continued ignorance, carelessness, and deception concerning these matters will no longer do. Malnutrition among our children must no longer be tolerated, for it only serves to perpetuate further the depletion of human immunity and general wellness. Let us follow the designs of our higher consciousness, ever aligned with nature, so that we at last may provide our future generations with healthier choices and our world with a more hopeful future.

Additional Thoughts About Immunity

Our immune system is designed to protect us from all micro-enemies, from within and without, primarily harmful bacteria, viruses, and various allergens. It is a complex, highly specialized system with one hundred million trillion antibody molecules, about a trillion lymphocytes (white blood cells), and an array of other chemical weapons such as interferon molecules, bone marrow, and spleen tissue, lymph nodes, and the thymus gland.

It has recently been established that we have three major types of T-cells (immune cells): *Killer T-cells*, obviously designed to attack invaders, *Assistor* or *Helper T-cells*, to help further or support the attack of the aggressor cells, and *Suppressor T-cells* that dampen the activity of various immune cells. The specialized message-sending of T-cells is performed by the release of chemical signals called lymphokines which send the message to attack, support, or retreat. The human immune system has great power, instinct, and diversity, but as great as this system is, it is directly affected by the foods we eat, the stresses we encounter, and ultimately the status of our human spirit.

Nearly two million people will die untimely deaths this year from combined heart disease, stroke, and cancers. According to our own governmental studies, nearly 60 percent of these often-preventable fatalities are directly related to diet. Currently, the emphasis still lies not with nutrition/immune education and disease prevention, but with profit escalation and marketing deception through brainwashing advertising and overdependency on pharmaceuticals, as well as hospitalization and research. And, as for health insurance, only a de-evolved culture would acquiese to a health insurance system which offers greater incentives for disease than the prevention of disease and wellness. Our priorities are perplexing as we appear more preoccupied with profitability from bacteria and viruses than with our own depleted immune system's inability to cope with them. All rewards, incentives, and profits are currently derived from, and dependent upon, sickness and disease.

Cancer and AIDS viruses, CMV (Cytomegalo virus), EBV (Epstein-Barr virus), mononucleosis, *Candida albicans*, genito-urinary tract infections, herpes simplexes, and frequently recurring potent strains of colds and flus seem to grow stronger, even as we grow weaker. Yet, there are still no federally funded campaigns to educate the public in a simple, understandable fashion about the general components, functions, likes, and dislikes of our precious immune systems, and the notion of preventive medicine remains but a faint shadow of what it should be.

In spite of information that continues to expose the health hazards of denatured foods, food additives, and processing techniques, we insist on using them in the name of pleasure, convenience, and profitability. It seems we have not truly realized that we have the power to radically improve the quality of human health and well-being. If we are to prevent disease, we must begin with sound nutrition. Good nutrition represents harmonization with nature, using natural foods to provide for the body's natural inherent needs. The American food industry continues to cover up and deceive, targeting not our best interests, but rather our obsessive compulsive weaknesses for sweets, alcohol, fatty foods, and salty fast foods for profit, as the average citizen, uneducated in nutrition, remains most vulnerable. It has all become very big business to sell us foods that play to our weaknesses and addictions which I believe may ultimately destroy our health. Furthermore, we are continually being manipulated and deceived by billion dollar slick advertising and manipulated by science-for-profit research.

We must take a hard look at where we are currently headed, with the intention of reordering our twisted priorities. But nothing short of a personal grassroots revolution is necessary if we are to stem the current tide of immune de-evolution—a revolution of personal awareness that ultimately affects each of our daily choices with respect to food, exercise, and medicine. As one person becomes educated about the realities of disease and prevention, his/her influence cannot help but to inspire a growing, rippling awareness. As the merits of such change begin speaking in greater volume, then the system must listen, and be forced to change as well. And perhaps it will come to pass that the system which once fed us will at last stop feeding off of us.

3

The Wu Way to a Natural Body

Before we can consider implementing any effective, preventive healing program, we should first refer to a time-tested model which teaches the interworkings between food and the human body. Moreover, in the spirit of true whole-ism, we should seek out a well-developed art/science that further addresses the delicate synchronicities between body, mind, and spirit and all the conditions of life that interconnect and affect them. As an advocate of true whole-ism and symbiotic interdependence, the Wu Way has been greatly influenced by the ancient healing model of Oriental medicine, a preventive system which applies nutrition as a healing art form. The Wu Way to a natural body represents a new wholistic approach to preventive healing and applied nutrition taken in large part from this very old standard. Before examining the new model, let us take a brief look at the timeless ancient healing model from which it derives much of its inspiration.

A Timeless Whole-istic Healing Model
Like most ancient cultures, the Chinese established a detailed system of whole-istic healing influenced by a core belief that all of life is infinitely interconnected. They referred to what we

call disease as disharmony and felt that all disharmony (disease) is due to the violation of nature's law resulting in and from the extremes of excesses and deficiencies.

The Wu Way recognizes the general system of Oriental medicine as but one example of a very effective preventive health care model, derived from ancients who exhibited a comprehensive understanding of nature and true whole-ism. It represents a system that evolved from six thousand years of observing nature and natural law. As with all ancient healing systems, the Chinese system relies in part on natural elements such as food, pure water, and herbs, in conjunction with the understanding of how the body systems respond in concert with the aforementioned elements as well as with each other.

The Wu Way embraces this reliance on the whole-istic systemic implementation of pure food and water as medicine and, with this in mind, feels strongly that applied nutrition is the most profound tool in the art of preventive healing. What's more, integrating applied nutrition with the whole-istic teachings of Oriental medicine establishes an even more dynamic healing model. It holds a key that opens the door to the "healer within."

Let us take a closer look at some of the primary basic teachings of Oriental medicine.

A. **The Five Fundamental Substances:**

(1) Chi–Life Force, or unseen vital energy field that protects and flows through and around the physical body.

(2) Blood–The *substance that food is converted to*. It is the primary transporter of nutrients. The stomach receives food and sends it to the spleen which distills (purifies/filters) it, converting it into blood.

(3) Jing–Life Source. The *essence fluids* of life: hormones, semen, etc.

(4) Shen–The invisible spirit within that charges or gives life to the life force (Chi).

(5) Fluids–Body fluids: sweat, saliva, gastric juices, urine.

These Five Fundamental Substances represent the fundamental substances of life which act as the criteria for wellness and disease. The Chinese, influenced by Taoist philosophy, ascribe to the principle that good health is a gift which can only result from proper understanding and harmony with natural law. The key to this maintenance is wisdom. Wisdom is the sole means by which one is led to proper understanding of the hidden workings of nature. Between and within all life systems from macro to micro, there are unseen laws or dictates governing the functioning of the universe, Earth, and Mother Nature, as well as the human body, mind, and spirit. This theory has infinite application extending to the most unsuspecting microcosms. It can be seen in the individual workings of all animal and plant life. Once one arrives at this understanding, he would then have the wisdom to harmonize with these laws and, thus, maintain the balance of the five fundamental substances.

B. **Microcosms** (places in the human body where the Five Fundamental Substances are to be harmoniously maintained):

(1) The Six Yang Organs (contractive which receive, break down and absorb the fundamental substances):

a. Gallbladder (Dan)

b. Stomach (Wei)

c. Small Intestine (Xiad Chang)

d. Large Intestine (Da Chang)

e. Bladder (Pang Guang)

f. Triple Burner (San Jiao)—unseen regulator for Lung/Spleen/Kidney

(2) The Six Yin Organs (expansive which produce, transform, regulate, and store the fundamental substances):

a. Heart (Xin)

b. Lungs (Fei)

c. Spleen (Pi)

d. Liver (Gan)

e. Kidneys (Shen)

f. Pericardium (Xin-Bao)—protective shield of the Heart

(3) The Six "Curious" Organs
a. Brain
b. Marrow
c. Bone
d. Blood Vessels
e. Uterus
f. Gall Bladder (both Yang and curious)

All the disharmonies are allowed by ignorance of the preferences of these body microcosms. In order for disharmony (disease) to reach pernicious (advanced) levels the two gates (inroads) must be invaded:

Predisposition–constitution, history, genetics.

Precipitation–sudden, abrupt, extreme influences.

With the Oriental system of healing, it is believed that each one of us is made up of different physical, mental, and spiritual natures, each influenced by a multitude of variables, including family, neighborhood, nature, climate, diet, etc. It is also believed that each of these variables is infinitely interconnected and, thus, subject to the same conditional natural laws of symbiosis. For example, crops are affected by climate, food nutrients are affected by cooking methods, and we are affected by all the above. The Wu Way feels strongly that the Oriental system of medicine provides us with a comprehensive model that seeks to eliminate the root systems or origins of disharmony. In so doing, it offers us a dynamic preventive system of healing.

The Origins of Disharmony are descriptively likened to climatic influences. Again, we must keep in mind here that nature within and nature without are seen as interconnected and symbiotic. Food is seen as one external influence that affects the internal climate of the body. For example, excess dairy creates dampness (mucus) in the spleen, and elimination or reduction of dairy resolves the problem. This is precisely how we may use food (nutrition) to prevent disharmony and thus heal.

C. **Origins of Disharmony**

(1) The six External Pernicious Influences of Disharmony:

a. Dampness (Yin/expansive)–affects the spleen downward: heavy, slow, bloated, thick, colored mucus/loss of appetite/ indigestion/abdominal edema/immune depletion from allergies, bacteria/phlegm/cold-chills.

This disharmony pattern is predisposed by a constitution that is allergic/mucusy with a history of chronic sinusitis/ rhinitis, chronic and acute immuno-suppressive disorders such as colds, flus, viral and bacterial infections, swollen lymphatics, edema.

Examples of damp agitating foods:

Cold (raw)	**Sweet**	**Phlegm Producing**
ice water, iced tea/coffee, fruit juices, fruit, milk, salad, sandwich, ice cream, frozen yogurt	sugar, honey, maple syrup, molasses, barley malt, fruit juices, fruit, alcohol	milk, cheese, yogurt (dairy), eggs, bananas, corn, wheat

Excesses of the above create disharmony (dampness or mucus) in the spleen.

b. Cold (Yin/expansive)–affects the kidneys: edema/frequent lower back pain/aversion to cold-chills/clear white urine/ clear mucus/infections and chronic or acute weaknesses in the genito-urinary tract: kidneys, ovaries, uterus, prostate.

The above dampness tends to bring cold to, and thus injures, the kidneys. The spleen rules the kidneys, so the above spleen disharmonies would generally apply here as well.

Examples of cold agitating foods:

Liquids	**Sodium**
water, juices, alcoholic beverages, soda/tonic/soft drink, coffee, tea	table salt, potato chips, pretzels, cottage cheese, feta cheese, packaged hams, deli foods, fast foods

Excesses of the above create disharmony (cold) in the kidneys

c./d. Heat/Fire (Yang/contractive)–affects the liver and heart: poisons in the blood that inflame and move upwards: acne/boils/carbuncles/red face/high fever/high blood pressure. Examples of heat/fire agitating foods:

Sweets	**Fats**	**Spicy** (hot)
any and all sugars, fruit juices, alcohol	red meats, cheese, whole milk, sour cream, oils, nuts, butter	hot pepper such as cayenne and jalapeno, tabasco, horseradish

Excesses of the above create disharmony (heat/fire) in the liver and heart.

e. Wind (Yang/contractive)–affects liver and lungs: sudden (acute) changes/tremors/dizziness/convulsions/twitching/tinitis/spasm/sudden-onset skin eruptions (rashes)/sudden-onset of contagious diseases.

The condition of wind is agitated by pre-existing disharmonies in the liver, spleen, and kidneys. Therefore, the patterns of disharmony in those respective regions of the body would apply here.

Examples of foods that must be avoided:

Sour/pungent foods: yogurt, lemon, lime, tabasco, coffee, chocolate, and food additives,

Excesses of the above create disharmony (wind) in the lungs.

f. Dryness (Yang/contractive)–affects lungs and bronchials: dry cough/asthma/bronchitis/scant urination/dry tongue/dry, impacted stools/thick, yellow mucus/excessive thirst.

The condition of dryness is agitated by pre-existing disharmonies. All the above Yang patterns apply here.

Examples of agitating foods that must be avoided:

Pungent foods: coffee, chocolate, sharp spices.

Excesses of the above create disharmony (dryness) in the lungs and bronchials.

Harmonizing (healing) Foods (natural application)
General examples of harmonizing foods:

Healing foods—cooked grains and vegetables (except corn and wheat in some cases) and vegetables or some other form of low-fat proteins.

Grains: oatmeal, brown rice, rye, millet, quinoa, amaranth, teff.

Vegetables: summer squash, green beans, kale, broccoli, winter squash, carrots, onions.

Sea vegetables (occasionally): dulse, arame, kombu, nori, hijiki, wakame.

Low-fat proteins: beans such as aduki, black, chickpea, kidney, lentil, mung, navy, pinto, soy, and turtle. Also tofu (bean curd), white fish, and occasional skinless, baked, or broiled poultry.

Use of the above foods will generally re-harmonize the body systems, and thus heal or offset the influences which initiated the symptoms agitated by excesses.

Six External Pernicious Influences of Disharmony

(physical disease)

The excesses create the disharmonious influences (disease) which in turn affect the organs are outlined as follows:

Food Excesses	Disharmonious Climatic Seasonal Influences	Organ Affected	Common Symptoms
Sweet Cold Mucus	Dampness	Spleen	Viral Infection Bloating/ Inflammation/ Phlegm
Salty Liquids	Cold	Kidneys	Bacterial Infections Chills/ Clear Mucus
Bitter Sweet Fat Spicy	Heat	Heart	Acne/Boils/ Fevers
	Fire		High Blood Pressure Yellow Mucus
Sour	Wind	Liver	Tremors/ Dizziness/ Spasms
Pungent	Dryness	Lungs	Dry Cough/ Asthma/ Bronchitis

The Five Internal Emotional Influences of Disharmony
The five Internal Emotional Influences when either excessively expressed or repressed affect the corresponding organ:

Emotion	Organ
Joy	Heart
Anger	Liver
Grief (sadness)	Lungs
Fear (fright)	Kidneys
Compassion/pensiveness	Spleen

There are actually seven influences: sadness being synonymous with grief and fright with fear.

Again, these emotional patterns influence and are influenced by the six aforementioned external patterns, i.e. food affects body and mind.

Within this same spirit, the Wu Way reminds us again that all chronic and acute disease (disharmony) patterns must pass through the two gates of influence: predisposition and precipitation. High blood pressure, therefore, must have a genetic or some other predisposition, but is often exacerbated by precipitating dietary and/or emotional conditions.

For further study of the system of Oriental medicine, I recommend *The Web That Has No Weaver* by Ted Kaptchuk, O.MD., and *The Yellow Emperor's Classic of Internal Medicine* by Ilza Veith. These are both exceptional books which the Wu Way relied upon as its main resources for the previous discussion on Oriental medicine. The Wu Way would also like to recommend the *Tao Te Ching,* an inspiring, age-old text that exposes the reader to the whole-istic philosophy of interconnectedness which inspired this system and the culture from which it emanated. This reading can be found in many different translations. Another book worth noting is *Tao: The Subtle Universal Law and the Integral Way of Life* by Taoist Master Ni,Hua-Ching.

The New Model

In order to restore the natural body, the Wu Way suggests we first make good nutrition a priority. Nutrition is designed to be an orchestration of forty instruments, delicately balanced, allowing for the symphony of nature to pass through each of our lives with resounding harmony.

There are forty nutrients that cannot be made in the body: fifteen vitamins, fourteen minerals, ten amino acids, and one fatty acid. From them our bodies synthesize over ten thousand different compounds essential to the proper maintenance of good health, via an estimated three thousand enzymes and co-enzyme compounds. Denatured foods have no place in the body's biochemical orchestration, for one discordant note can initiate a systemic upset of the natural rhythm of our bodies, opening the door to disease. In addition, when redesigning our food plan, we should make a commitment to avoid generally most of the food additives which threaten our health and immune well-being. We should also limit expanded food variety which can severely tax our digestive processes, serving to ultimately weaken immunity. The Wu Way appeals to our common sense, sensitivity, and ultimately greater discipline and knowledge in order that we may opt for healthier choices.

In more specific terms the Wu Way first suggests a thorough reading of all food labels. It is most important that we identify any potentially harmful unnatural ingredients in our foods. As an aid there are a number of food additive dictionaries to help us determine whether a given food product is laced with additives which are best avoided. A good reference that comes to mind is *A Consumer's Dictionary of Food Additives* by Ruth Winter, published by Crown Publishing of New York. We must be prepared to reduce overall fat and sugar consumption, as well as table salt and/or foods high in sodium.

The Wu Way suggests we avoid "junk foods" and overuse of highly fermented foods, such as pizza, beer, and marinated foods, to mention a few. Basic bacterial immunity is more easily maintained when excessive sweets and fermented foods are not overconsumed, as they can upset the ratio of harmful-to-protective bacteria in the intestines. More specifically, the Wu Way suggests that we study the list of sweets and fermented foods (see Wu Way Undesirable List below) in order to avoid excessive use. It is important to note here what the Wu Way calls its 85 percent Rule. Given the nature and demands of our current lifestyles, it is recommended that we allow ourselves 15 percent dietary leeway. Although it may seem that the need for perfection is implied, the Wu Way feels that the notion of perfection is suggested for illness of an obsessive nature. Therefore, to simply do your best approximately 85 percent of the time is more aligned with the Wu Way's natural teachings.

We might also refer to a good basic guide such as the aforementioned "Dietary Goals for the United States," the Senate subcommittee recommendations published by the U.S. Senate in January 1977. This report may be purchased in the form of transcripts through most major public libraries for a nominal fee. The report's recommendations read as follows:

Current Diet	**Dietary Goals**
16 percent saturated fat	10 percent saturated fat
26 percent poly- and monounsaturated fat	20 percent poly- and monounsaturated fat
2 percent protein	12 percent protein
22 percent complete carbohydrates	40-50 percent complete carbohydrates
24 percent sugars	15 percent sugars

The Wu Way Undesirable List
A. Avoid/Limit

All sugars: sucrose, dextrose, glucose, maltose, corn sweeteners, turbinado sugar, raisin syrup, honey, maple syrup, molasses, and anything made with these sugars.

Any and all fried foods.

White flours and processed carbohydrates in general, including: white rice, buns, rolls, sweet rolls, doughnuts, pizza, crackers, chewing gum; cake, cookies, ice cream, white flour pasta; soft drinks (diet or otherwise; sugar-free or otherwise); sweetened fruit juices, non-diluted fruit juices; condiments such as mayonnaise, ketchup, relish, jellies, jams, and gravies; excessively fatty foods including sour cream, cream soups, and chowders; alcoholic beverages of any kind, and caffeinated drinks of any kind.

B. Limit:

Yeast—beer, wine; yeasted supplements—yeasted breads (substitute sour dough breads); mushrooms; vinegar (substitute lemon/lime or Cardini's salad dressings); soy sauce, tempeh, miso, tamari (substitute Braggs sauce); coffee, tea; most packaged products and commercial condiments— substitute brands free from above ingredients where possible or prepare your own at home.

Goal Number 1: To increase complex carbohydrate consumption to account for 55-60 percent of the energy intake.

Goal Number 2: To reduce overall fat consumption from approximately 40 percent to 30 percent of energy intake.

Goal Number 3: To reduce saturated fat consumption to account for 10 percent of total energy intake, and balance with polyunsaturated and monounsaturated fats, which should each account for about 10 percent of the energy intake.

Goal Number 4: To reduce cholesterol consumption to about 300 mgs a day.

Goal Number 5: To reduce total sugar consumption by almost 40 percent so that it accounts for no more than 15 percent of the total energy intake. (Also to restrict all highly processed sugars)

Goal Number 6: To reduce salt consumption by about 50-85 percent to approximately three grams per day.

These goals suggest the following changes in food selection and preparation:[1]

(1) Increase consumption of fruits and vegetables.

(2) Decrease consumption of meat and increase consumption of poultry and fish.

(3) Decrease consumption of foods high in fat and partially substitute polyunsaturated fat for saturated fat.

(4) Substitute nonfat milk for whole milk.

(5) Decrease consumption of butterfat, eggs, and other high cholesterol sources.

(6) Decrease consumption of sugars and foods high in sugar.

(7) Decrease consumption of salt and foods high in salt.

Both the food additive dictionary and the subcommittee dietary goals report help us with our commitment to read labels with a greater sense of conviction and awareness as we set up these new parameters. Furthermore, you may simplify your plan by choosing to avoid any label indications or chemical additives that you cannot pronounce. Perhaps simplistic, but a safe rule of thumb. That which nature provides is usually easy to pronounce! The Wu Way feels it is most important to refuse to buy foods with chemical additives or excess/added sugar, salt or fat, accenting the need to get back to the basics as nature intended. The Wu Way continually reminds us of the importance of our commitment, awareness, and vigilance throughout this endeavor.

Once we have focused on more natural wholesome foods such as fresh fruits and vegetables, we still have to deal with the problem of insecticide sprays. The Wu Way, to neutralize these poisons, is to use an acid-to-alkaline rinse. Simply purchase two 16-ounce spray bottles at your neighborhood hardware store and fill each of them with 15 ounces of tap

---

[1]Michio Kushi, *The Book of Macrobiotics: The Universal Way of Healing and Happiness,* (Tokyo: Japan Publishing Inc., 1983), p. 168.

water. In one bottle add one teaspoon of apple cider vinegar; in the other bottle add one teaspoon of baking soda. Label them both and keep them readily available. Next, a natural bristle brush and a colander are needed. Simply spray your produce first with the cider vinegar solution, then with the baking soda solution. Finally, brush the produce briskly, place in the colander and rinse with tap water. This simple method will both cleanse and neutralize many of the insecticide residues and poisons that coat the fresh produce. Even though there are a number of other methods, I have always found this one to be the simplest and most convenient.

Now that we have taken care of fats, sugars, salt, additives, and pesticides, what of food allergies or intolerances that are presented by the de-evolutionary cornucopia syndrome? As described in Chapter Two, the simplest, most accessible means to identify food intolerances may be with what the Wu Way calls Acu-Vedic (AVK) and/or various other systems of Behavioral Kinesiology (BK).

Exploring the Secrets Held Within Our Muscles— The Anatomy of the Human Energy Field

The hard science of applied kinesiology, founded by Dr. George Goodheart, has its roots in chiropractic medicine and focuses on pure physiology. By definition, applied kinesiology is the study of muscles and how muscle groups interact with each other as well as with corresponding glands and organs. On the other hand, behavioral kinesiology, popularized by Dr. John Diamond, places prime importance on the everchanging etheric sensitivities of the subtlest human responses, taking into consideration emotion, feelings, and reaction to changing stimuli. The Wu Way has further adapted its own form of kinesiology called Acu-Vedic Kinesiology (AVK) because it integrates elements of the aforementioned influences with acupressure (derived from the ancient, internal Chinese art of acupuncture extending back forty-five hundred years), and the Ayervedic (derived from India) science of Chakra energy. The Wu Way's Acu-Vedic Kinesiology

(AVK) system utilizes a number of the over one thousand imperceptible trigger (acupuncture) points existing on the fourteen meridian grids that generate the electromagnetic force field in and around the body. It also employs the use of the 7 major and 21 minor Chakra points or major energy zones radiating from within all the major glands and organs (See Figures 1A and 1B). These ancient systems believe that all primary "life force" energy followed a sequential metabolic path passing from these unseen Chakra (body energy zones) to the seventy-two thousand nadis (nerve endings) onto the nervous system (impulse pathways), endocrine system (glands and organs), and finally the skeletal-muscular and blood systems in an ordered time sequence (See Figure 2). Here we can also see an example of the Wu Way's teaching that all subtle life force energy transits from soft/internal to hard/external or mind to body (psycho to soma). To paraphrase the classic whole-istic law of cure stated by Herring, all disease emanates from the inside out, and from the head down. Therefore, the sequential, metabolic life force path moves from: mind perceptions to...thought impulses to...the central nervous system to...the peripheral nervous system to...the autonomic system to...the endocrine system and finally to...the skeletal-muscular and blood systems in a timed sequence (See Figure 3).

Acu-Vedic Kinesiology (AVK), for the purposes of this book, will simply resemble the Behavioral Kinesiology (BK) system founded by Dr. John Diamond. The uniqueness and amplification of AVK as a system of kinesiology will not be fully discussed in this work but will be explored in detail in a later book on this topic. Use of AVK and/or BK in allergy testing, while quite simple, has proven to be profoundly accurate. Once an individual is exposed to an allergen, the first reaction is often "unseen" or subtle. It may be as simple as a feeling of general weakness or malaise that results from a lessening of the body's electromagnetic force. This life force, termed "prana" by the Ayervedics, and Qi (Chi) by the Chinese, keeps the "spirit"

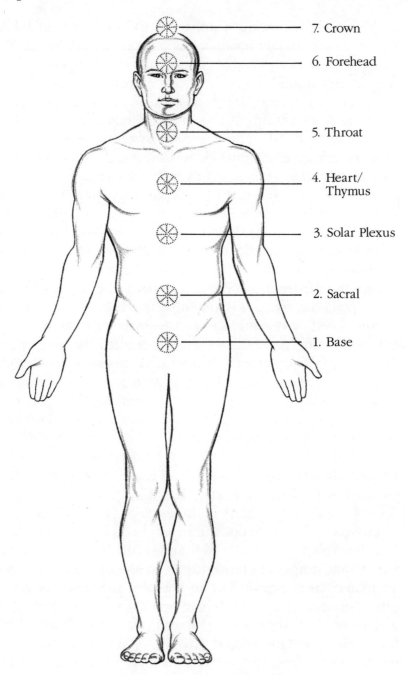

7. Crown

6. Forehead

5. Throat

4. Heart/ Thymus

3. Solar Plexus

2. Sacral

1. Base

Figure 1A – 7 Major Chakras

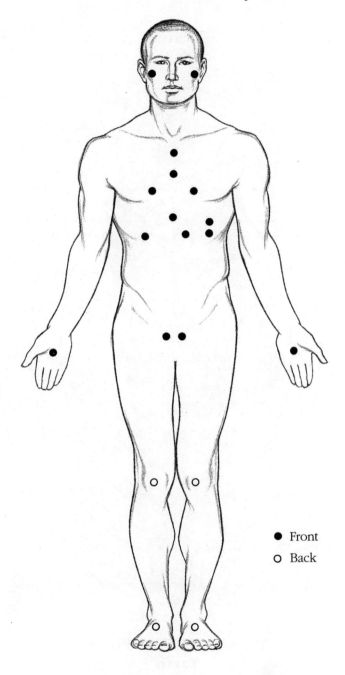

Figure 1B – 21 Minor Chakras

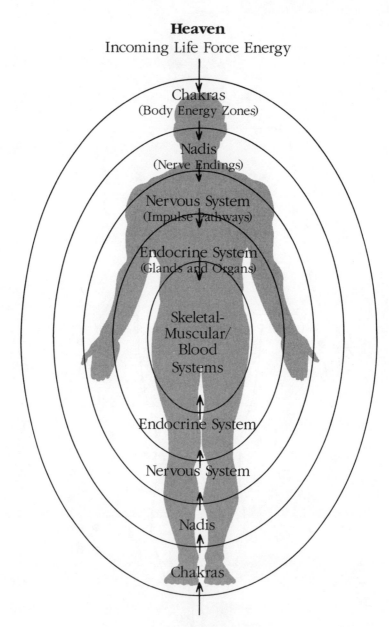

Heaven
Incoming Life Force Energy

Chakras
(Body Energy Zones)

Nadis
(Nerve Endings)

Nervous System
(Impulse Pathways)

Endocrine System
(Glands and Organs)

Skeletal-
Muscular/
Blood
Systems

Endocrine System

Nervous System

Nadis

Chakras

Incoming Life Force Energy
Earth

Figure 2 – Metabolic Life Force Path

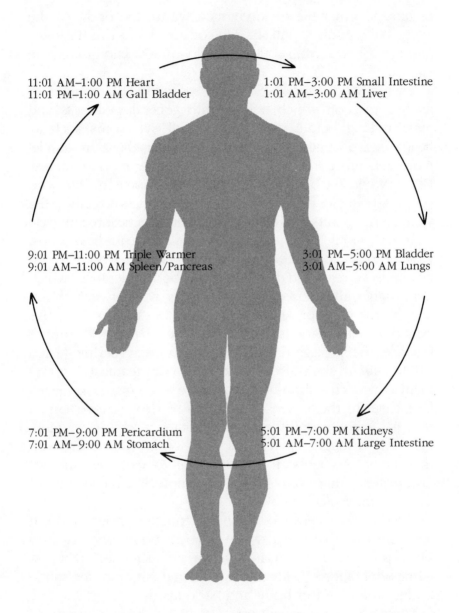

11:01 AM–1:00 PM Heart
11:01 PM–1:00 AM Gall Bladder

1:01 PM–3:00 PM Small Intestine
1:01 AM–3:00 AM Liver

9:01 PM–11:00 PM Triple Warmer
9:01 AM–11:00 AM Spleen/Pancreas

3:01 PM–5:00 PM Bladder
3:01 AM–5:00 AM Lungs

7:01 PM–9:00 PM Pericardium
7:01 AM–9:00 AM Stomach

5:01 PM–7:00 PM Kidneys
5:01 AM–7:00 AM Large Intestine

This chart was adapted from *Tao, The Subtle Universal Law and the Integral Way of Life* by Taoist Master Ni, Hua-Ching, p. 48.

Figure 3 – Time Transits of Energy Through the Body Systems

or unseen inner life force charged within the body. As the allergen temporarily pulls the plug on and drains this life force, there is a short-term, subtle but profound reduction in muscle vitality.

It is really quite simple. Someone eats a food that triggers an allergic reaction which begins with general weakness and malaise long before the next level of symptoms such as headaches, dizziness, and vomiting appear, there are subtle, more general reactions such as weakness or mood changes. Here is where the body's vital energy points come in. One need only hold samples of suspected foods or extracts directly to the vital energy points–to interrupt electromagnetic force (muscle resistance)–to determine force field intolerance to these foods. Expose foods to unseen pressure points on the body to see how muscles react and thus determine food intolerances which may trigger allergic reactions?–you may wonder. Before you dismiss the concept, keep in mind the fact that for forty-five hundred years various ancient cultures have held similar practices in high regard, with thousands of years of time-tested validity. Remember, also, that despite our steadfast commitment to modern techno-medicine, there still remains no means for measuring the presence of, or response from, subtle human energies (emotion/spirit) on any computer, machine, or graph. It is only through ten years of professional counseling with thousands of clients, in what I like to call my "life art observatory," that I've come to fully appreciate the validity of this revealing procedure!

AVK is an esoteric system based on the ancient Eastern teaching that there is a dense physical body responsive to seven primary subtle bodies within, characterized by a systemic orbit of force fields that pass in and out, from the subtle bodies to the denser body, and back again.

There are many ancient practices that developed articulate spiritual references for these unseen selves or interconnected subtle bodies. These theories, which date back thousands of years, postulate that there are seven major unseen human energy fields surrounding all living bodies, each of which is uniquely separate though interrelated. (See Figure 4).

In the West we essentially feel that humans have one body. These "subtle bodies" theories embraced by many ancient Eastern cultures tells us there are no less than seven major unseen human bodies or energy fields.

The Major Seven are:
(1) Etheric Body (Genito-Urinary)
(2) Emotional Astral Body (Abdomen)
(3) Mental Body (Pancreas)
(4) Pure Astral Body (Thymus)
(5) Etheric Template (Thyroid)
(6) Celestial Body (Brain)
(7) Soul Body (Pineal)

Each of these represents unseen energies that are believed to relate to, and are prerequisites for, the "life force" system in all living beings. The first two etheric energies are described as the primary subtle energies emitted by human life; all other energies are secondary. Ether energy is the essence energy, the primary manifestation of aliveness.

The Etheric Body is said to be the first layer just outside the physical body; this subtle body corresponds with the first Chakra. There is also an etheric fluidium which is thought to be the energy connection from the etheric body to the physical cells. The Emotional Astral Body is the second outer layer of energy outside the etheric body; it is a force tied to subtle emotional energies, capable of manifesting as pure emotion even after physical death. It is said that any severely imbalanced emotions unresolved in the physical life are far more intensified in the Astral Body after death. It corresponds with the second Chakra. The Mental Body represents the energy embodiment of thought attached to the physical body existing as an energy field just outside the Emotional Astral Body. This body corresponds with the third Chakra. The Pure Astral Body is the

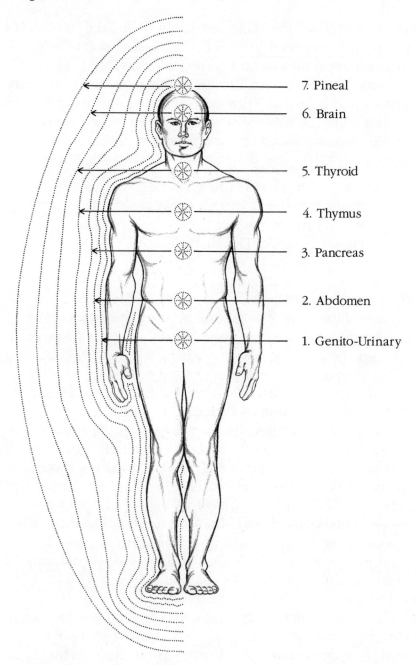

7. Pineal

6. Brain

5. Thyroid

4. Thymus

3. Pancreas

2. Abdomen

1. Genito-Urinary

Figure 4 – The Anatomy of the Human Energy Field

next energy layer existing outside the Mental Body consisting of pure, intensified human emotional energy. This body corresponds with the fourth Chakra. The next layer is the Etheric Template. This body both supports and bridges an energy connection between the Etheric Body and the physical cells. This body corresponds with the fifth Chakra. The next subtle body is the Celestial Body, which is simply the lighter spirit body which manifests as pure thought energy of a higher order. This body corresponds with the sixth Chakra. The final major subtle body is the Soul Body, described as the primary life force or battery body, the clearest, simplest, purest, highest manifestation of "self." This body corresponds with the seventh Chakra.

The above descriptions were adapted from a myriad of sources including *Flower Essences and Vibrational Healing* by Kevin Ryerson, published by Brotherhood of Life, Albuquerque, New Mexico and *Hands of Light* by Barbara Ann Brennan, Bantam Books. The Wu Way suggests that the above texts be consulted for further reference and study.

Many ancient spiritual systems begin with the premise that all humans, animals and plants share and recycle unseen energy, manifest in an array of force fields surrounding their denser physical body. In *Future Science,* author John White enumerates ninety-seven different names for this auric phenomenon from nearly one hundred different cultures. Of late some theories have gained acceptance here in the West with newly coined terms such as "bio-currents," "body electric," "bioenergetics," and "energy fields."

Most of this recent awareness in the West was inspired from holistic healing systems with Eastern influence such as: Seichem, Johrie, Omega, Jin Shin Jyostu, and Reiki. The ancient Taoists believed that human beings had a "five-fold body." They felt that we combined our "physical body" with a "body of pure universal law," a "subtle body," a "crystal body," and a "great harmonious body," with some of us adhering more to subtle law with a greater spiritual energy, and others clinging to more formative earthly energy.

Exactly like the magnetosphere force field that surrounds the Earth, all living things macro to micro possess this same force field. That is to say, force fields surround the earth, all her living organisms, and even their individual, micro-internal structures. AVK and/or BK are primarily concerned with the forces within and passing through separate internal organ structures, macro and micro.

Many healing systems that originated in the East were based on the belief that there are unseen, but measurable, magnetic morphic force fields in and around the body. It is somewhat like checking the life of a battery within a flashlight. The varying degree of life within the battery cell, though not visible, ultimately determines the level of energy transfer. It is the intangible, invisible aspect of this work that makes it so difficult for deductive Western minds to understand or accept.

In the systems of Oriental and Ayervedic medicine, the body's energy points correspond with various endocrine glands and vital organs within, which, according to these ancient systems, hold the key to the levels of harmony and/or disharmony of those respective glands and organs. These systems are not intended to be of diagnostic value in the traditional Western medical sense, but rather in a much more subtle etheric, energy sense. Sensitive (weak) liver point response may merely suggest that there is a lessened vital energy or life force in the liver area uncovering a pattern of disharmony. This pattern, when further traced down, will often exhibit unhealthful dietary trends, behaviors, and tendencies that are subtly weakening the organism. It does not necessarily suggest any serious liver disease or ailment.

Since the beginning of time, humans have recognized that there is clearly an etheric force that differentiates a vibrant body from a languid body. With life there is an unseen force, a spirit, an invisible force field, if you will, that keeps a radiating warmth within the stimulation of vital fluids. This force, though invisible to the human eye and elusive to the practical mind, remains compellingly the greatest and most powerful energy known to man—the force of life or "life force." The ancient Egyptians called it "Ki;" the Chinese, "Qi" (Chi), the ancient Indian, "prana."

Any discussions of "life forces" or unseen "human morpho-magnetic force fields" is most unnatural to our way of thinking and therefore requires some consideration of physics.

"In Newtonian physics, all causation was seen in terms of energy, the principle of movement and change.

All moving things have energy—the kinetic energy of moving bodies, thermal vibration and electro-magnetic radiation—and this energy can cause other things to move."[2]

Einstein took it a step further. His physics tells us that electrons and various atomic nuclei are electrically charged, creating specific spatial patterns predetermined by time and space, which in turn ultimately predetermine the unique, though clearly interrelated, electromagnetic force field structures. These structures serve to further potentiate and predetermine the extended probability for additional unique, though still interrelated, manifestations of energy, ad infinitum.

In addition, we might consider the hypothesis of formative causation established by the Cambridge and Harvard scholar, author Rupert Sheldrake, who terms this "life force" phenomenon the "radio-like transmission of invisible, intangible vibrations through the electromagnetic field,"[3] influenced by what he calls "morphic resonance."[4] The principle of this hypothesis is that supranatural structures from pre-existing systems, continually affect the genesis of subsequent interrelated sys-

---

[2] Rupert Sheldrake, *A New Science of Life. The Hypothesis of Formative Causation,* (Los Angeles: J.P. Tarchor Books, 1987), pp. 59-60.

[3] ibid, p. 123.

[4] ibid., p. 95.

tems cumulatively predetermined by space, time, and unique energetic adaptation.

All of this genius simply serves to remind us that everything is unique yet interrelated with and affected by everything else, even as with the very thought process that takes us from deductive to inductive, from sequential to spatial, from worldly science to universal philosophy, from man to God. We are all specific, unique, organized, reactive masses of energy; life forms with glands and organs which also exist as separate unique energies, influencing and influenced by spatial patterns and various magnetic fields from micro to macro on an endless continuum.

The ancients knew that where there was life, there was life force. What they lacked in hard science, they made up for in spatial awareness. They were observers and recorders of life systems and life forces, life force transfers and adaptations.

When contemplating such issues, early man simply relied upon right brain thought, more creative, more sensitively attuned to internal feelings, sense perceptions, and intuitions. These natural cultures laid the foundation for our discovery of the unseen human force field, but they did not only contemplate this life force. For centuries they studied and graphically detailed the specific orbital patterns of this energy and the vital exit/entry points between the subtler, etheric, and denser physical bodies. This study gave birth to natural healing arts and their hybrids such as acupuncture, Jin Shin Jyutsu, shiatsu, acupressure massage, Reiki, Omega, Johrei, Seichem, and Acu-Vedic and/or Behavioral Kinesiology.

When we examine such phenomena more closely, as did the Taoists, we see that flow patterns of magnetic force move from all the vital glands and organs out through the skeletal muscular system, radiating outside the body and circulating back in again in a specific ordered time sequence. "Many phenomena clearly demonstrate that individuals are not awarenesses residing in the head areas of their physical bodies but are interrelated fields of energy to which the skin presents no barrier at all."[5] The basis for this electricity is the transitory "electric wiring," provided by the seventy-two thousand "nadi" or nerve networks that pass from head to toe. Though the ancients laid the foundation for this information, modern science has had occasion to delve a bit further.

A great deal of scientific research in this area has recently been done in the West. Yale University's Harold Burr, M.D., spent at least thirty years researching the steady energy dynamics of living organisms with a voltmeter, the results of which are detailed in his book, *The Fields of Life*. What Dr. Burr clearly demonstrated in his work is that plants, animals, and human beings indeed do possess electromagnetic force fields which determine and are determined by the form and condition of the organism to which they belong. One of Burr's colleagues, Dr. Ravitz, a psychiatrist, used Burr's voltmeter to study the energy dynamics of human emotions. Ravitz found measurable electromagnetic force field variations associated with corresponding human emotions.

Of the number of contemporary scientists who have added to this research, perhaps the most outstanding are Dr. Bjorn Nordenstrom of Sweden and Dr. Robert Becker of the United States. Dr. Nordenstrom's work is described as follows:

> Dr. Nordenstrom is an internationally recognized scientist with over 30 years research experience. A specialist in radiology, Nordenstrom pioneered the needle biopsy, a diagnostic technique now used in every major hospital in the world. More important, however, has been his two decades of research into the bioelectric fields of the body, studies which culminated in the book, *Biologically Closed Circuits: Clinical, Experimental and Theoretical Evidence for an Additional Circulatory System*. In terms of conventional medicine, this book is revolutionary, and naturally it has been ignored. Nordenstrom's major thesis is that the

---

[5] W. Brugh Joy, M.D., *Joy's Way*, (Los Angeles: J.P. Tarciter, Inc., 1979), p. 122.

body contains a complex electrical system that regulates the activity of the internal organs and is the foundation of health. Nordenstrom backs his thesis with two decades of meticulous scientific research. He claims that modern medical science has not adequately explored the electrical properties of the body and has yet to explain how the chemical and physical processes of the body are interrelated.[6] (Drs. Nordenstrom and Burr's work is further elaborated in the book noted by Footnote 6).

Maybe the American scientist best known for bridging this gap between East and West is Barbara Ann Brennan. She has an M.S. in Atmospheric Physics from the University of Wisconsin and is most noted for several years of project work for NASA at the Goddard Space Flight Center. Brennan's background in the hard sciences makes her book *Hands of Light, A Guide to Healing Through the Human Energy Field* a convincing account of the human force field which may be of noted interest to the doubting scientist. Currently there is a wellspring of information coming to the forefront regarding the human energy field.

Once properly understood, these points and meridians provide a healing artist with numerous possibilities. For example, if a patient has a sluggish liver and an acupuncturist places the acupuncture needles on a corresponding liver point, this may open up a magnetic channel as a sort of "jump-start" designed to stimulate the sluggish liver with additional "chi" or "life force." Similarly, AVK and/or BK make use of this unseen human internal energy network to observe endocrine disharmonies and various systemic intolerances which may occur from, among other things, improper diet.

Both the ancients and contemporary bioenergeticists believe that all reactions proceed from the subtle to the gross, or from

---

[6] Clark A. Manning and Louis Vanrenen, *Bioenergetic Medicines East and West, Acupuncture and Homeopathy,* (Berkeley, CA: North Atlantic Books, 1988), pp. 15-16.

the "soft internal" to the "hard external." This means that all disease and healing begin as a subtle magnetic reaction long before they manifest in the material body. This follows the ancient Chinese interpretation of the Twelfth Law of Change of the Infinite Universe. All physical manifestations are Yang contracted/soon to expand (immaterial) at the center, and Yin expanding to material at the surface.[7] Just as when a stone is dropped into a pool of water, the ripple effect always moves from internal to external. With allergic reactions, long before the patient notices external symptomology, internal changes are taking place in subtler forms.

After one eats an allergy food, the first feeling is a general malaise or a weakness. One who practices this bioenergetic kinesiology ascribes to the belief that the muscles hold the clue to allergic reactions via the unseen life force. For it is this life force that must either activate or vacate the muscles, depending on the influence of the exposure. Thus, instead of eating a food that we would classify as an allergen and then measuring the body's weakened or allergic response, we can actually take that same food, expose it to a vital magnetic pressure point, and check the degree of resistance exhibited by the muscle. If the food in question has a positive effect on the muscle's strength upon vital point exposure, it may then be assumed that it has a positive effect on the force field or life force, or whole person, in general. If the food has a positive effect on the life force, then we may assume it is well tolerated as a liferendering food. On the other hand, if the muscles are weakened, it is assumed at that point that the food is not well tolerated by the subtle energy bodies and is therefore a depletor of the life force which ultimately extends to the denser physical body.

While "kinesiology" refers to the scientific study of muscles, AVK and/or BK refer to the study of the interrelationship between muscles and the life force, and between the life force

---

[7] Michio Kushi, *The Book of Macrobiotics: The Universal Way of Healing and Happiness,* (Tokyo: Japan Publishing Inc., 1983), p. 7.

and various external stimuli, such as foods, beverages, vitamins, minerals, clothing materials, drugs, exogenic and environmental allergens. Many applications and theories stem from this telling work, and much debate stems from its etheric nature. Yet, there exists a great deal of documentation as to its validity. Dr. John Diamond, founder of the Institute for Behavioral Kinesiology in Valley Cottage, New York, continually researches this subject and publishes ongoing scientific findings. Dr. Diamond's research group publishes a monthly newsletter, which may be obtained by contacting the Institute for Behavioral Kinesiology in Valley Cottage, NY. However, for readers to test themselves for subtle energy food sensitivities at home they must first have a basic understanding of the technique. Let us examine this technique further.

The deltoid muscle, which is an anterior/medial/posterior muscle articulating at the shoulder, is the primary test muscle because it is generally the most accessible. For the purposes of at-home AVK and/or BK testing, the deltoid muscle is referred to as the indicator muscle. Two people are needed to administer this test properly.

(1) Both must stand face to face, properly squared off at approximately an arm's length.

(2) Both must assume proper erect posture, with head straight forward and erect, shoulders back and down, feet comfortably positioned in line with shoulders and parallel to the ground.

(3) The subject must raise his/her left arm at shoulder height, firm the arm, and make a fist while maintaining the correct posture with the right arm still comfortably relaxed at the side.

(4) The other person will simply place his/her left hand on the subject's right shoulder and his/her right hand on the subject's extended left arm just above the wrist.

(5) Let the subject know that you are ready to push down on his left arm, asking him to resist with all his strength.

(6) Now push down on the arm quickly with a firm, even force. Keep in mind that your intention here is simply to test the spring in the subject's muscle, not overwhelm or fatigue it. This is not a competitve test of strength (See Figures 5A and 5B).

We are now ready to test the subject for a variety of foods. Begin by first compiling a food group master list that you can use for reference in future tests, since food sensitivities detected by muscle testing change from time to time depending on a great many factors. Your food group master list should contain relevant foods from all the primary food classifications (See Wu Way Food Classification List on pages 104 ad 105). The foods most suspected for sensitivity are the favorite, most frequently consumed, or any unusual new foods recently introduced that may be of suspicious origin. Take inventory in the refrigerator, cabinets, and cupboards of your kitchen; whatever pertinent foods are not on hand may be put on a grocery list. Once you have the basic testing technique mastered, the master food list drawn up, and all the foods you wish to test available, you are ready to begin testing.

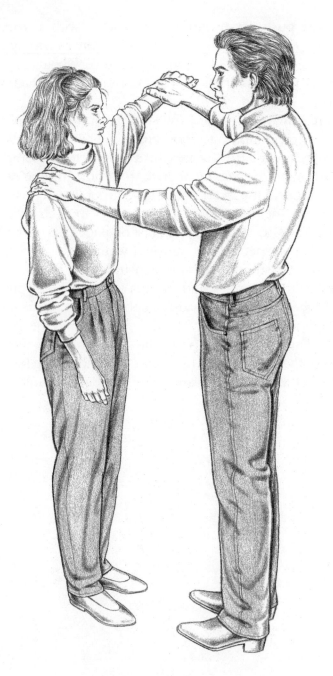

Figure 5A – Muscle Test Figures

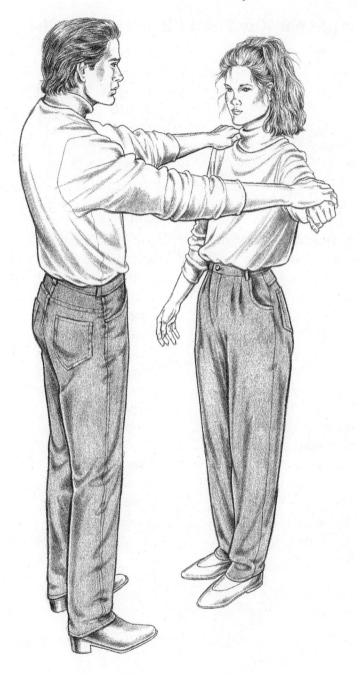

Figure 5B – Muscle Test Figures

Sample Wu Way Food Classification List

Proteins
chicken
clam
cod
crab
flounder
halibut
ham
lamb
lean beef
liver (beef and chicken)
lobster
pork
salmon
sardine
shrimp
sole
tuna
turkey

aduki
black beans
chickpeas
kidney beans
lentils
mung beans
navy beans
pinto

almond
Brazil nut
cashew
macadamia
peanut

Proteins (con't)
pecan
pine nut
pistachio
sesame
sunflower
walnut

cheese
milk
soy—tofu, Pacific
soy milk, Sun soy milk
yogurt

Sugars
barley malt
brown sugar
cane, maple & rice syrup
honey
turbinado
white sugar

Fats
avocado
butter
coconut
cream
lard
margarine
vegetable oil

Sample Wu Way Food Classification List (con't)

Low & Non-Starch Vegetables

asparagus	
bok choy	
broccoli	
Brussels sprouts	
cabbage	
cauliflower	
celery	
Chinese cabbage	
collard	
eggplant	
endive	
garlic	
green beans	
kale	
kholrabi	
lettuce	
mushroom	
okra	
onion	
parsley	
pepper	
radish	
sorrell	
spinach	
sprouts	
summer squash/ zucchini	
Swiss chard	
turnips	

Starches

beet
carrot
chestnut
corn–aglutella wheat-free
  corn pasta
globe artichokes
Jerusalem artichokes
lima beans
parsnip
peas
potato
pumpkin
winter squash
yam

Grains

amaranth–cereals & pastas
barley
brown & white rice, Food for Life
buckwheat–SOBA
millet–quinoa–quinoa pasta
oats–oatmeal, oatbran cereal
rye–cream of rye cereal
teff
triticale
wheat–cream of wheat

Sample Wu Way Food Classification List (con't)

Acid Fruits	**Sub-Acid Fruits**
grapefruit	apple
kumquat	apricot
kiwi	berries (blue, black, raspberry)
lemon	cherry
lime	grape
orange	mango
strawberry	nectarine
tomato	papaya
	peach
Melons	pear
cantaloupe	plum
casaba	tangerine
Christmas melon	
honeydew	**Sweet Fruits**
muskmelon	banana
Persian	date
watermelon	fig
	all dried fruit

For specific testing, you and your subject assume the proper posture described for the basic testing technique, in a room free from the interferences of television sets, radios, stereos, and microwave ovens. Instead of the subject's right hand remaining relaxed, it must hold the food to be tested next to his/her body, exposing the food to three vital life force energy points successively. Point One is between the eyes, Point Two is where the second rib joins the breastbone in the upper mid-chest area, and Point Three is just below the navel. We will refer to these points as (1) Brain, (2) Thymus, and (3) Abdomen points (See Figure 6). As each food is exposed to each of these primary energy points, there will either be an unyielding muscle, indicating a positive tolerance to the food being tested, or a muscle unable to resist, indicating a negative intolerance. As you progress down your food list, draw a line through the

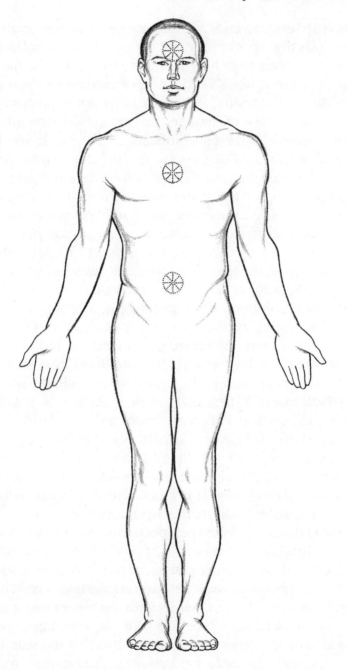

Figure 6 – Three Vital Life Force Energy Points

foods that seem to elicit an intolerance response and circle those foods that appear tolerable. Be sure to allow at least five seconds between tests for the muscle to recoup. Neither the subject nor the tester should smile or converse to any great extent during the testing. Also remember not to push so hard as to fatigue the subject's muscle. This not a test of strength. The muscle strength is not as significant as the subtle life force indicated within it. The muscles remain the communicative medium between these subtle etheric messages and the denser human physiology. It is also essential to limit food testing to no more than twenty minutes or one hundred tests at any two sessions, and not to exceed more than one session per day. As the testing proceeds either the tester or a third party should keep track of all the tolerated and untolerated foods. This list will give the subject a specific, individualized, up-to-date analysis of foods from which to establish a healthy diet. AVK and/or BK testing provide us with a most valuable insight, isolating those foods which are most digestible and, therefore, supportive of vital life force. Each master food sheet should be dated and kept in a folder for updates and maintenance.

Disclaimer: Kinesiologic muscle testing is not intended to be a diagnostic assessment and should in no way be used to replace the efforts of a skilled licensed diagnostic physician or allergist. Also, persons with a history of structural bone and muscle or chiropractic problems should avoid this procedure as it could induce pain, discomfort, and further symptomatology.

To bring things back into perspective in our Wu Way Natural Body Healing plan, we must fully appreciate the impact of such individualized food testing and use this information to elevate our level of nutritional awareness and application. The Wu Way reminds us that this plan begins with the commitment to the use of clean, minimally processed, low-fat, low-sugar, low-salt foods as nature intended. Remember also that the reading of labels, the use of simple food additive dictionaries, and the familiarization with basic recommendations from the "Dietary Goals for the United States" Senate Subcommittee findings of January 1977 provide us with good, sensitive, and sensible parameters for re-evolutionizing bodily wellness.

Once you have established your commitment to natural food and modified your food chart, having encircled the foods you have tested well for and crossed out those your muscles tested weak for, you are ready to assemble your Wu Way meal plan.

General Wu Way Meal Plan

The sample below is to be designed in accordance with the final results of the muscle tests, recorded on the Wu Way Classification List.

Breakfast: (approximately) 1 cup hot whole grain cereal, 1 teaspoon crude unrefined oil high in mono- and polyunsaturates (Example: canola oil).

2 ounces of 1 percent lactate milk or lowfat soymilk

Mid AM: 1 fresh fruit (usually sub-acid).

Lunch: (approximately) 6 ounces protein with 6-8 ounces vegetables, 4 ounces starch (usually whole grain products, such as brown rice or whole grain pasta).

Mid PM: (approximately) 6 ounces garden salad, diced raw vegetables (dress salad with 2 tablespoons canola oil mixed with lemon/lime and herbs), with 1/8 cup seeds or nuts.

Dinner: (approximately) 6 ounces protein with 6-8 ounces vegetables and 4 ounces starch.

Evening: 8 ounces plain low-fat yogurt.

The above sample is general and will vary in accordance with more specific individual needs.

Note the recommendation of hot whole cereal grains for breakfast. The Wu Way takes into consideration that throughout most of man's one million year history on this planet crude unrefined grains and breads comprised 60 percent of his total caloric intake. Grains were and still are the staple food on all continents, easy to prepare by boiling or making into unleavened breads, and always easily stored in burlap sacks without fear of spoilage. So the Wu Way recommends approximately one cup of cooked cereal grains for breakfast (whole brown rice or cream of rice, cream of rye, oatmeal, etc.) as well as approximately four ounces of additional whole grains or whole grain pastas with lunch and dinner. Aside from the high content of B vitamins, trace minerals, and fiber, these optimal carbohydrate sources provide the body with a balanced supply of abundant energy. The Wu Way does not recommend many deviations from the suggested breakfast. Juices are very concentrated, highly processed food extractions, higher in their concentrated sugar yield than most people are aware. In general, the liver cannot metabolize more than 50 grams of sugar at one serving; four ounces of fruit juice delivers approximately 120 grams of sugar!

We need not have Ph.D.s in nutrition to follow the Wu Way to a natural body plan. In most cases, our natural common sense will provide solutions to the nutrition problems created by modern de-naturalization. As we learn to apply our natural common sense with greater sensitivity, we will provide ourselves with more trustworthy answers. Sweet rolls, juices, doughnuts, bacon, sausage, and sugar-sweetened processed cereals, as we've come to know them, provide tasty breakfast options. They are, however, so far removed from nature that their only value lies in taste and convenience. On the other hand, more complex food questions may arise. For example, if eggs are found to be tolerated through muscle testing, and if digestion is good and cholesterol is known to be within normal range, two eggs eaten twice a week should be considered acceptable. Also, sourdough, yeast-free, or unleavened breads are generally more favorable because the less agitation from fermented foods that assist potentially dangerous proliferation of invasive anaerobic bacteria in the large intestine, the more efficiently the human immune system functions. Not only does the Wu Way recognize unleavened bread as a more natural option, it further emphasizes that many colds, flus, and immune disorders may ultimately be traced back to rampant invasive bacterial proliferation, triggered in part by excessive fermented foods such as yeasted bread. Rather then trying to cure a cold or flu, it is far better to prevent them, and the best way is to stop feeding the invasive, unfriendly bacteria in your large intestines with fermented foods.

Another food that might be consider here as a breakfast option is plain low-fat yogurt. Again, provided it appears to test properly and there are no known serious intolerances, yogurt may act as a good low-fat protein-carbohydrate breakfast food, with the potential for immune support. The acidophilus/lactobacillous strains (healthy fermentations) actually increase the living flora and fauna bacterial life population in our intestines, which enhances our bacterial immune-support. A simple 8-ounce serving of low-fat plain yogurt may be added to any Wu Way breakfast plan one to two times per week, especially during the warmer months of late spring and summer. Ancient Taoist teachings tell us the spleen is sensitive to excessively sweet and cold foods especially during the cold, damp seasons of winter and early spring. This is because mucus originates in the spleen and is the by-product of excessive cold dairy foods such as yogurt. That is why it is most important to implement muscle testing, which enables us to check the body's subtle response to a specific food, such as in this case, yogurt.

For mid-morning snacks, one serving of fruit is recommended, usually sub-acid because it is generally more easily digested. Again, this will vary with muscle testing and individual needs, but the Wu Way sees the merit of limited fruits in the meal plan especially during the cold season. We are encouraged to select fruits based on seasonal and native availability and generally to avoid the overly sweet tropical fruits. All fruits are living foods, with high digestive enzyme counts capable of assisting in digestion and detoxification.

Fruits and vegetables continue to oxygenate (live) long after they are harvested, unlike flesh foods which oxidize quickly after the slaughter. Fruits and vegetables are also high in potassium and vitamins A and C, to mention but a few important nutrients. But as discussed earlier, the Wu Way also teaches that our ancestors used only a limited supply of indigenous, seasonal fruits. Only with the advent of modern transportation and refrigeration has man been able to change all that. Nowadays, of course, fruit is readily available and many nutritionists and authors currently espouse programs that sing the praises of excessive fruit usage. While some people may derive health benefits for a limited period of time from such programs, the Wu Way does not recognize fads or shortcuts as a truly natural means of healing. Natural seasonal yield and the spleen's sensitivity to excesses of cold and sweet should be two good reasons to discourage the overuse of fruit. Periods of excessive stress that may create a hypersensitivity in the adrenal glands, pancreas, and/or liver would be seen as times when one might also benefit from abstinance from fruits, as they may contribute to "spacey," anxietal, or neurotic hyperactive behavior by raising sensitive blood sugar levels in the brain.

The Wu Way regards lunch and dinner as major mealtimes when one should make use of protein, vegetable carbohydrate, and, in most cases, starch. The approximate four to six ounces of low-fat protein, again extracted from your test list, should *predominantly* consist of either (1) vegetable proteins if and where possible; beans, (aduki, chickpeas, lentils, etc.); tofu (soy curd), soybeans, soy grits; (2) fish; or (3) poultry. These proteins should be baked, broiled, steamed, boiled, or *lightly* stir fried.

The approximate six to eight ounces of vegetables should be fresh and preferably organically grown to ensure freedom from insecticides. If organically grown vegetables are not available, you may wash the vegetable first with an acid (cider-water) solution, then rinse and wash with an alkaline (baking soda-water) solution, and rinse under the tap. Now your lunch and dinner vegetables are ready for steaming, one of the preferred ways of preparation. Steaming will provide a greater alkaline mineral and enzyme yield, although occasionally light stir frying in an iron skillet will tend to yield trace iron, as well as an additional variety of acid minerals.

For the most part, the Wu Way sees some vegetables as less desirable than others, although foods are digested uniquely in each human body. No two vegetables are digested the same, no two fruits, etc. Each of us possesses entirely different digestive capabilities, some better than others, subject to change at various times in life depending on an array of issues. It is therefore recommended that muscle testing serve as the ultimate criterion for all food usage. As one looks to heal or improve body wellness, they may benefit in a more general sense from avoiding excessive use of vegetables that are considered more difficult to digest. Among them are nightshade vegetables (containing belladonna residues) such as cabbage, Brussels sprouts, peppers (red/yellow/green), eggplant, broccoli, and cauliflower. Potatoes, yams, and sweet potatoes are also nightshade vegetables but are generally far less difficult to digest. Belladonna is a naturally occurring poison, which, at its worst, usually causes no more than some minimal digestive gas, but is capable of causing a number of health complaints, among them arthritis, eczema, psoriasis, fatigue, and immune depletion. Not unlike potatoes, yams, and sweet potatoes, tomatoes are also considered a nightshade food better tolerated than most. Tomatoes are, however, classified as an acid fruit, not a vegetable.

Other potentially harmful foods that one might limit include mushrooms, sprouts, peanuts, pistachio nuts, and melons, which contain fungus and mold capable of increasing the populations of harmful intestinal bacteria. In addition, other allergic food by-products include acetaldehyde, formaldehyde, gallic acid, oxalic acid, quercetin, anthocyanide and uric acid.

Almost all foods contain at least some potential food allergens or naturally occurring chemical substances that may, in some cases, prove toxic. For example, corn contains acetaldehyde, crab meat contains gallic acid, cashew nuts contain anthocyanide, and cherries contain uric acid. It is important to note here that the degree of potential toxic reaction ranges from barely noticeable and harmless to severe anaphylactic. The exact degree of avoidance is dictated entirely by individual chemistries. While most relatively healthy people will not need to be concerned with such strict dietary adherence, these restricted foods are mentioned primarily for those who wish to use nutrition as a primary tool for preventive medicine. For those who choose to use foods for healing, there is little margin for error. You'll need every edge you can get. The Wu Way attempts to give you that edge.

Mid-afternoon snacks should consist of approximately six ounces of raw diced vegetables or a garden salad. This limited supply of raw vegetables helps to provide raw enzymes, undisturbed by heat from cooking, which help to digest the preceding lunch and initiate digestion for the dinner ahead. With the raw vegetables, one may use a yogurt dip with herbs. For the garden salad, one may combine two tablespoons of olive oil, canola oil, or some other crude, unrefined vegetable oil containing healthy mono- and polyunsaturated fats, together with lemon/lime juice, or liquid whey with added herbs, to make a healthy dressing. Also, various brands of vinegar-free dressings are also sold at most health stores. Remember, vinegars are unfriendly bacterial instigators! Along with the raw vegetable snack, the Wu Way recommends a small handful of nuts or seeds selected in accordance with individual muscle test results. Sesame seeds, sunflower seeds or almonds, and sesame (tahini) butter, sunflower butter, and almond butter spread on rice cakes or Ryvita-type yeast-free, wheat-free rye crackers, all represent sources of raw vegetable protein with the potential to help most people sustain blood sugar/energy levels at this low-energy time of the day. Perhaps the best low-fat alternatives are the delicious, easy-to-digest soy cheeses and cream cheeses.

Mid-afternoon is a time when many of us suffer our most significant drop in blood sugar. We have been up since early morning meeting the rigors and stresses of the day. In this mid- to late afternoon period we tend to feel tired, hungry, low in energy, and unclear in our thinking. These dense snack foods help offset the drop in blood sugar with their sustenant amino acids and vegetable fats.

In some cases, the Wu Way recommends using plain low-fat yogurt for the evening snack. If well tolerated, and there appears to be no "dampness" from the spleen (excessive mucus), it represents a superior immune food, especially during the spring and summer seasons. Yogurt is also an ideal food before bedtime because it is predigested. That is, it contains a high enzyme count, along with living cultures, which enable it to digest itself at a time when the body's digestive efforts are winding down. It is light, yet sustaining; it is also three times as rich in calcium as any equivalent dairy product. This ready supply of calcium and naturally occurring whey can help ensure a restful sleep.

If the reader is interested in tailoring a specific nutritional plan that takes overall health and caloric intake into consideration, then he should consult a qualified professional nutritionist. General information can also be found on the back pages of the popular paperback entitled *The Nutrition Almanac,* which gives a comprehensive breakdown of recommended calorie intakes adjusted to gender, age, status, etc.

Wu Way Food Combining

The General Wu Way meal plan is not intended to be a nutritional therapy. The Wu Way does acknowledge, however, that a more comprehensively designed nutrition program may in some cases be used as a primary therapy and a dual therapeutic adjunct with traditional Western approaches. In certain instances where a person is in poor health and in need of nutritional support, the Wu Way strongly suggests a professionally designed monitored program, similar to the one outlined here, with additional attention paid to specifics such as the proper combining of foods. Proper food combining is a powerful tool of nutrition that really need only be applied when health has been markedly impaired. Proper combinations of foods are believed to digest efficiently when taken at the same meal, whereas all improperly combined foods may upset healthy digestion and nutrient assimilation. This theory is based on the idea that all foods digest at a rate correlating with the density of their molecular composition. Denser protein molecules from meat are generally more difficult to digest than lighter, easier-to-digest carbohydrates from celery. So one rule of food combining tells us that we must not take two different protein foods per meal, like the shrimp cocktail appetizer with the beef main course. All that density from two separate sources unnecessarily burdens the digestive system. Another rule of proper food combining tells us that it can be equally trying for our digestive systems to take two different fast-oxidizing, lighter carbohydrate-rendering foods. That is, if we were to combine a fast-oxidizing plum at the same meal with a non-starch carbohydrate like broccoli, it is likely that we may trigger fermentation, creating digestive duress. The specific enzymes required to break down each of these foods will, in fact, create digestively incompatible excesses of fermenting nitrogen, methane, hydrogen, or gas in the intestines.

Over the years there have been many studies substantiating the validity and value of proper food combining, most by notably Dr. Herbert M. Shelton, who from 1928 to 1981 compiled the most extensive research data on the topic. Dr. Shelton's research was first noted in 1924 in the *Journal of American Medicine* by Dr. Philip Norman, who supported the theory of proper food combining, citing its effectiveness and validity as a science. My professional experience leads me to concur with this theory. I see continuing evidence of the remarkable healing power of proper food combining, noting its especially dramatic effects on patients whose etiology is directly traceable to digestive/metabolic disorders. The Wu Way tells us to consult our common reasoning, reminding us that, if we so choose, we can make common sense of this complex food combining issue quite easily.

Remember that our ancestors were considerably limited in the foods available to them. Keep in mind they lacked resources, such as refrigeration and transportation, which also limited food variety. For one million years, primitive natural man foraged for and farmed only those indigenous foods from his immediate surroundings, which were supplied seasonally by nature. If it was out of season or did not grow where you were, you simply did not eat it. Improper food combining is but one modern by-product of the de-evolutionary spiral. Though technology has provided us with the means to store and transport a wider variety, and thus availability, of foods, our digestive systems are paying the price. The Wu Way Food Combining Chart helps us to make use of the nutritional healing tool of proper food combining (Figure 7).

For a broader view, the Wu Way suggests that we become familiar with the food rotation system employed by nature. Again, keep in mind that natural man was never concerned with rotation of foods. Nature, with its changing seasons, provided man with a specific rotational harvest in accordance not only with the seasons, but also with the climate. For a better understanding of all this the Wu Way encourages us to study resources such as *The Fox Fire Book/Fox Fire 4*,[8] which help us to gain a far better understanding of how natural man planted and harvested in harmony with all the forces of nature. In these books, we not only see how the seasons and climates

---

[8] *The Fox Fire Book* and *Fox Fire 4*, (Gavan City, NY: Anchor Books/Anchor Press/Doubleday, 1972 & 1977).

The Wu Way Food Combining Chart

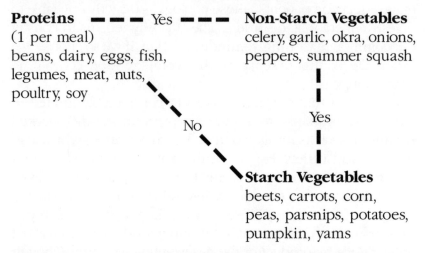

Proteins — — — Yes — — — **Non-Starch Vegetables**
(1 per meal)   celery, garlic, okra, onions,
beans, dairy, eggs, fish,   peppers, summer squash
legumes, meat, nuts,
poultry, soy

No   Yes

Starch Vegetables
beets, carrots, corn,
peas, parsnips, potatoes,
pumpkin, yams

Acid Fruits	**Sub Acid Fruits**	**Sweet Fruits**
citrus, pineapple,	apple, apricot,	bananas, currants,
kiwi, strawberry,	berries, cherries,	dates, figs, raisins
tomato	grapes, oranges,	
	nectarine, papaya,	
	peach, pear	
(taken alone)	(taken alone)	(taken alone)

Rules
1. Only 1 protein taken per meal.
2. Do not combine proteins with starches.
3. Do not combine fruits with any other foods or
   any fruit groups.
4. Proteins combine well with non-starch vegetables.
5. Non-starch vegetables combine well with starch vegetables.
*Chew all food well.
*Take all beverages before or two hous after meals—
never during

Figure 7– The Wu Way Food Combining Chart

influenced planting, harvesting, and dietary rotation, but also the phases of the moon, planets, and stars.

The Wu Way also directs our attention to the Ancient Chinese Five Phase Element theory, 500 B.C. (See Figure 8). which depicts a system devised by primitive/natural man, interrelating natural universal elements and energies. This, too, reflects a system of food rotation coordinated with nature. In both of these examples we see food rotation in harmony with nature, as well as simple food selection, which naturally allows for a greater degree of digestive harmony.

Combining foods properly from the list prepared by accurate muscle testing wields a most powerful healing influence. It helps to keep personal records as one attempts to heal his body the Wu Way. Keeping notes on how certain foods affect us at different times is most helpful for re-tests and updates. And, as mentioned repeatedly, common sense and sensitivity will always serve you well along the path of the Wu Way. Finally, it is most important to note again that the Wu Way is in *no way* designed to act as a replacement for a qualified health care practitioner.

Summary

It is essential that we learn to assume greater responsibility for ourselves. The Wu Way personalized approach may help your body get back in touch with its inherent needs and thus increase your probability for body wellness. Yet, as the Wu Way has stated throughout, everything is universally interconnected, bound by universal law. Just as disease is systemic, so too is wellness. And, just as the body relies on physical support like good, clean, digestible food and exercise for wellness, the body, mind, and spirit all continually rely on each other for wellness. Each represents a system within one unified integrated system, separate yet interdependent. The first ancient universal principle of the infinite universe, translated by ancient Chinese sages, is: "Everything is a differentiation of one infinity." The universe works perfectly. If man chooses for his body to work

The Five Phase Element Chart
(The Universal Elements and their Related Qualities)

Element: Wood
Season: Spring (active phase)
    Grains: wheat, barley, oats, rye
    Veges: broccoli, leafy greens, green squash, string beans
    Fruits: tart fruits
    Beans: lentils, green split peas
    Animal Foods: chicken

Element: Winter
Season: Winter (transitional phase)
    Grains: kasha, buckwheat
    Veges: seaweeds, sea veges
    Fruits: blackberry, blueberry, cranberry, concorde grape
    Beans: black beans, kidney, pinto, adzuki
    Animal Foods: bluefish

Element: Fire
Season: Summer (peak phase)
    Grains: corn, summer squash
    Veges: kale, escarole, hickory, mustard greens
    Beans: red lentils
    Animal Foods: shrimp, lamb

Element: Metal
Season: Autumn (declining phase)
    Grains: rice
    Veges: onions, cabbage, turnips, celery, radish, cauliflower
    Fruits: pears, apples
    Beans: soybeans, tofu, navy beans
    Animal Foods: haddock, turkey, beef

Figure 8 – The Five Phase Element Chart

Element: Earth
Season: Indian Summer (neutral phase)
        Grains: millet
        Veges: winter squash, yams
        Fruits: sweet fruits
        Beans: chickpeas
        Animal Foods: swordfish, tuna, pheasant

The above chart is in reference to a temperate climate such as is found in the United States, Canada, and Western Europe.[9]

---

[9] Annemarie, *Food and Healing,* (New York: Ballantine Books, 1986), p. 86.

well, then he must learn once again to work in harmony with the universe. Awakening his "whole-istic" innateness is the first step on the Wu Way to human body wellness.

While it remains essential for each of us to evolve personally in a microcosmic sense, it is also essential for all mankind to re-evolve more wholistically in a more global way. I see the sudden emerging proliferation of personal and global problems manifesting as violated laws of nature demanding compensation, reminding us that we have no choice but to return to harmony with natural law. For each of us human body de-evolution exists in a microcosmic sense because of systemic human desensitization. I believe that one major reason AIDS and cancers are on the increase is that human immune capability is declining, paralleling our de-evolving quality of life. This human immune decline can be seen merely as one broken spoke on a weakened wheel on a wagon speeding out of control. Just as we have turned our backs on the pivotal relationship between ourselves and nature, all that is attached to that pivotal point will be affected in kind. Polluted water and air, ever-increasing levels of stress, contaminated food, dependence on a health care system that relies almost exclusively on drugs and hospitalization, the nutritional poisoning from insecticides and additives are all symbolic of our divorce from nature. Furthermore, these are symbols of choices we have made along the way–choices born of greed, fear, and chaos. Choices derived from an isolationistic progress that arises from the human ego, as a drive to rise above the inherent laws of nature. We continue to opt for technology, shortcuts, short-term pleasure, and convenience.

As the toll from all this de-evolutionary fallout continues to mount, our options are diminishing. As our bodies continue to suffer, let us be reminded by our pains that the unnatural de-evolved world we have created has failed. Let us, then, be inspired to make a new commitment back to Wu Wei (Nature). As we look to make our bodies well, let us do so with a "wholistic" spirit of healing, sensitive to and more aware of the miasms (etiological patterns) that show us how we got here from there. Then, without blind faith, false promise, or panacea, let us rise up and take new "old" steps, reflective of good choices that stem from good conscience, common sense, sensitivity, and courage of conviction.

4

The Unnatural
Human Mind

The Brain/The Mind

It is generally accepted among philosophers and scientists that
the human brain is a gland in that it produces hormones and
contains hormone receptors. Without exception, every single
activity the brain engages in involves hormones. With this in
mind, it is important to remember that regulatory hormones
are found throughout the body along with magnetic force fields
which are found all around the body. Thus, the once inconceiv-
able idea of thinking taking place outside the brain is now
considered plausible by most experts. This seemingly enor-
mous conceptual gap, which for centuries separated our
perceptions of body and mind, has closed and once again we
have returned to the type of "whole-istic" body-mind principles
espoused by great ancient philosophers such as Plato, Aristotle,
and Socrates more than two thousand years ago. This theory
of systemic body-mind physiology simply will not go away. As
we think, we feel; as we feel, we think; as we think we feel,
we feel. It is all inseparable. The relative perception of the life
process for better or for worse begins in the mind and is then
transmitted by hormones and electricity through the brain,
ultimately reaching the body reflexes and influencing both

125

behavior and physiology. Expansive thought energy transits outward, influencing behavior and, ultimately, physiology. In accordance with this ancient philosophy, thought ultimately manifests as form. As one lies awake at night, worrying fearfully over a loved one who has yet to return home safely, the body metabolism accelerates in response to emotionally induced central nervous stimulation, which in turn interferes with sleep. Soon, pyruvic and lactic fatigue acids accumulate in the muscles, causing stiffness, joint pain, and achiness. The mind first perceives, then transmits through to the body—they are as one.

Our minds exist both independently of, and in synergy with, our brains. The human brain is defined as "a mass of nerve tissue in the skull of animals designed to facilitate intelligence and understanding." The mind, on the other hand, is defined by Webster as "that which in man makes him a creature with consciousness and intelligence." The mere use of the word "mind" clearly implies the subtle human presence of what we call spirit- or soul-self associated with the human experience. The brain, on the other hand, suggests the mechanics and biology of thought. Yet, they function as one.

Dr. Herbert Benson tells us the human brain contains more than one hundred billion nerve cells, each with numerous tentacles or dendrites and axons that, during brain activity, communicate with each other continuously. These communication connections, called nerve synapses, in effect are actually electromagnetic neurotransmitters with regulatory hormones and hormone receptors. All ideas, insights, and brain messages are sent through this process of neurotransmission synapse. The limitlessness of this system is staggering and so is the potential for ideas, insights, and brain messages. With approximately one hundred billion nerve cells, each of which has between one thousand and five hundred thousand connections, and with each brain cell connection possessing the potential to communicate with any other cell connection in the brain, the number of possible connections in the brain is astronomical.

How many connections are possible? Stated as a number, it's 25,000,000,000,000,000,000,000,000,000,000. Put another way, if you stacked up on your desk standard sheets of typing paper, one on top of the other, an amount equal to the number of possible brain connections, that stack would extend beyond the moon. It would extend beyond the planet Pluto. It would extend beyond our galaxy, and even well beyond the known limits of the entire universe, about 16 million light years away.[1]

The Major Parts of the Human Brain (See Figure 9)

(1) The Brain Stem consists of the mid-brain, the pons, the medulla, and the spinal cord. It is considered the oldest part of the human brain and is thought to deal primarily with breathing, heart rate, and alertness.

(2) The Cerebellum and Brain Stem regulate complex voluntary muscle movements.

(3) The Limbic System (the animal brain) regulates eating and drinking, sleeping and walking, body temperature, balance, and pituitary function. It also facilitates memory, emotion, and a higher order or spirituality.

(4) The Cerebrum organizes, remembers, provides communication skills, appreciation, and creative skills.

The primary divided human brain is called the Cerebral Cortex and was finally complete in its formation about 100 million years ago. This outer layer cortex consists of several major areas:

the occipital lobe (vision);

the temporal lobe (hearing, perception, meaning);

the parietal lobe (sensory body information); and

the frontal lobe (planning, decision making, purposeful behavior).

---

[1] Herbert Benson, M.D., *Your Maximum Mind*, (New York:Random House, 1987), p. 25.

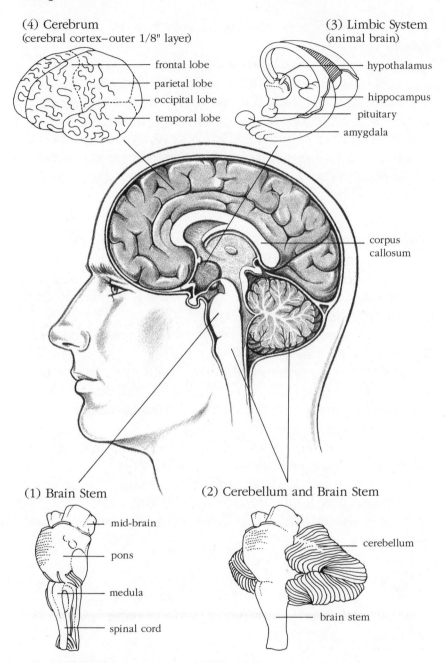

(4) Cerebrum
(cerebral cortex—outer 1/8" layer)

frontal lobe
parietal lobe
occipital lobe
temporal lobe

(3) Limbic System
(animal brain)

hypothalamus
hippocampus
pituitary
amygdala

corpus callosum

(1) Brain Stem

mid-brain
pons
medula
spinal cord

(2) Cerebellum and Brain Stem

cerebellum

brain stem

Figure 9 – Major Parts of the Human Brain

All talents and skills as well as mathematics and problem-solving are synthesized in the cortex which is largely comprised of the neocortex, which did not fully develop until about one million years ago. The cortex is divided into two separate parts—right and left—each with its own separate characteristics and control of human behavior. Between these two distinctly different brain centers lies the corpus callosum, which carries impulses from side to side, enabling the two hemispheres to work in concert.

As remarkable as this "human computer" is, it is highly sensitive and, in fact, disjointed from many of the influences of modern day living. At the National Institute of Mental Health in Bethesda, MD, the Head of the Laboratory of Brain Evolution and Behavior Dr. Paul MacLean states,

Man finds himself in the predicament that nature has endowed him essentially with three brains, which despite great differences in structure, must function together and communicate with one another. The oldest of these brains is basically reptilian. The second has been inherited from the lower mammals, and the third is a late mammalian development, which...has made man peculiarly man.

Author Arthur Koestler informs us,

The "reptilian'" and "paleo-mammalian" brains together form the so-called limbic system which, for the sake of simplicity, we may call the "old brain," as opposed to the neocortex, the specifically human "thinking cap." But while the antediluvian structure at the very core of our brain, which controls instincts, passions and biological drives, has been hardly touched by the nimble fingers of evolution, the neocortex has expanded in the last half-million years at an explosive speed which is without precedent in the history of evolution.[2]

---

[2] Arthur Koestler, *Janus, A Summing Up,* (New York: Random House, 1978), pp. 9-10.

The manner in which modern man's mind has evolved has entailed so much planning, scheming, and deductive thought that a great deal of his animal instincts, emotional awarenesses, and sense of higher order has been all but forgotten. All that now remains is a mind that reflects a highly imbalanced brain. As we have evolved or de-evolved, as it were, from agrarian to industrial and finally to technological beings, real problems have arisen from the type of thinkers we have become as well. Modern man is now more clearly dominant in his "new brain." Furthermore, far beyond this neocortex development, he has truly taken on a mind of his own. As we have de-evolved, we have adopted a de-evolved modern mind-set where the human doingness has all but totally replaced the most natural elements of our innate human beingness. The brain of modern man reflects an imbalanced, troubled mind.

The Split Brain

As mentioned earlier, in recent years neurophysiologists have further explored "split brain phenomena," or the belief that the human brain has two distinctly separate, differently functioning parts. These two divergent brain hemispheres are classified as "right" and "left." Actually, accurate terms might be "dominant hemisphere" and "inferior hemisphere" because the difference in brain functioning is influenced by whether or not a person is right- or left-handed. For our purposes, we will simply refer to this split brain phenomenon as right and left brain.

The left brain operates analytically with logical, deductive reasoning, and is in charge of all language and verbal skills. It categorizes and edits constantly, striving to problem-solve and make sense of vast amounts of both new and stored information. Deductive left brain thought always reasons sequentially from the general to the specific. Since this is the primary mind-set of our modern technological world, we see ourselves constantly seeking to control ever-expanding problems, groping to make them smaller, simpler, and more understandable. The more we see that this is not always possible with left brain thinking alone, the more out of control we feel, and the more inclined we are to react instinctively with fear. This gives rise to furthering the obsessive/compulsive control response which typically includes addictive, desensitizing behavior. The Western mind with its dominant left brain obsession to solve, control, and dominate problems grows ever more overwhelmed by the expanding magnitude of today's uncontrollable de-evolutionary crises: overpopulation, pollution, nuclear proliferation, etc. This futile scenario is naturally followed by the adoption of denial systems which often culminate with obsessive-compulsive gratification and addictive tendencies.

As compulsion seeks to control, addiction seeks to release. Ours is a highly controlling, addictive culture. As many as eighty million lives are affected directly or indirectly by alcohol abuse, sixty million by sexual abuse, and many more through drug abuse. Recently it has been estimated that fifteen million families are abusively violent. Some 60 percent of women and 50 percent of men in this country have eating disorders. And while it is nearly impossible to accumulate accurate data on workaholism and sexual addiction, their numbers are clearly beyond calculation.

While it is important to emphasize the magnificence of both the left and right brains, it is clear that when the brain's hemispheres are out of balance, the resultant unnatural mind will display various forms of neuroses and/or extensive behavioral disharmonies. On the other hand, when both hemispheres are balanced, the human mind may reflect the natural symbiotic model it was intended to be. The Wu Way acknowledges a profound need to balance and heal our troubled minds. This is first achieved with greater emphasis on right brain awareness and development which may serve to counteract our excessive left brain influences. We can initiate this process by observing the behavior of more natural, primitive brain-balanced cultures.

The right brain is the intuitive, creative, artistic center. It is the place where we sense without limit or boundary and where we possess the ability to perceive things spatially. More important, it holds the key to our ability to change and grow, ever expanding beyond the limitations of ingrained habits and thought processes. When we speak of mind limitlessness, we are speaking of the right brain. We have all heard of fire walkers, people who reach higher mental states, walking over hot coals without experiencing pain or burns. We have also heard of ESP, telepathy, faith healing, and the like. We hear stories daily of major behavioral changes through positive mental attitude that result in weight loss and broken addiction patterns. These are but a few examples of right brain phenomena and its boundless potential.

The Disappearing Balanced Brain/
The Lost Natural Mind

When we study ancient, more "natural" agrarian cultures, we generally see more balanced behavior, clearly in part due to a simplicity of lifestyles where there is greater attunement to nature around and within. Reliance and respect for one's inner nature is manifest in right brain thought. Whether we are speaking of the American Sioux Indians, the Ancient Taoists, the Hunzakuts of Northern Asia, or Aboriginal Tribes from Australia, we see an innate connection with the spirit of Mother Nature and natural self, which has gradually vanished with most industrial and technological societies. This intuitive natural thinking appears to be one vital missing link between modern man and a more balanced healthy mind. It is where ancient man affirmed the cooperative link between his unseen etheric self, affixed to the spirit of all that surrounded him, and his logical self. It not only exercised a higher consciousness, but a healthier conscience. Ancient man was more brain-balanced; he was more naturally evolved with his internal and external environments, and thus, he was better adjusted mentally and emotionally.

The Native Americans are perhaps the best example of this wholistic symbiosis. Rooted by family and tribe, grounded by the Earth, and spiritually reverent toward all that lived, these early Americans were at one in body, mind, and spirit. Their minds were uncluttered by industrial technology, choosing to live by the dictates of nature; their right brains were fully developed by art, mysticism, and ancient transcendental spirituality. Their mental-emotional balance serves as a lesson in stark contrast to our modern day madness. There is something very healing about feeling a sense of belonging. This healing strength derived from the warm "security blanket" of belonging to tribe, nature, and universe and surely contributed largely to the mental, emotional, and spiritual stability of these Native Americans for they were a culture deeply and reverently aware of their interconnectedness with all creation.

The Cherokee tradition celebrated the interrelationship of everything in creation. They revered the Earth as Mother, "Mon-o-la," the sacrament of God's presence. Whenever a Cherokee had to take an animal for food, he would always pick the weakest and the smallest of the herd, so the remainder would grow strong. In showing his sacred appreciation for interconnectedness, he would justify his hunt with a prayer to the Great Spirit (Creator), asking for forgiveness.

Their minds were naturally balanced, and reflected behavior of a higher order. They were adept in left brain survival and problem-solving techniques. Knowing well how to hunt, farm, and build well-adapted housing structures in cooperation with nature, they never compromised their right brain transcendentalism which embraced universal interrelatedness.

In the saga of his early Cherokee boyhood, *The Education of Little Tree*, Forest Carter tells a story that illustrates the creative, right brain "spirit mind" of the Cherokee. It is a story told by his grandmother. Her father, named Ground Hog, had a special relationship with trees.

He could hear "tree thought." His trees were beautiful, and they weren't at all selfish. They allowed ground for sumac and persimmon and hickory and chestnut to feed wild animals. Then one day Ground Hog saw loggers high in the mountains figuring out their plan to cut down these beautiful white oaks. Ground Hog said that the trees began to cry.

The lumbermen built a road to bring their wagons into the mountains. The Cherokee protected the trees. At night after the loggers left, the Cherokee men, women, and children dug trenches across the roads. In the day time the loggers would come and fill the trenches. Then one day, a white oak fell across the road destroying a wagon. After this, the lumbermen stopped trying to build roads, and left the white oak in peace. At the next full moon, the Cherokees celebrated. They danced and the white oaks sang and touched their branches together and touched the Cherokee. Grandma said they sang a death chant for the white oak who had given his life for the others.[3]

The Indian was in harmony within his mind and heart, and thus nature.

It was in large part due to his spiritual/natural mind connection with nature that the Native American functioned with such whole-istic success. Even when nature decided not to co-operate with him, he would go deep within his spirit/ right brain to rise above such limitations, in meditations, dreams, and prayers, for he knew this creative brain represented great power as it crossed over from the physical into the spirit realm. "After more than 25,000 years of occupancy, the Indian left the land as rich, as wild, and as beautiful as his immigrant ancestors had found it. He was a resounding ecologic success. For him, the primeval forest, the virgin

---

[3] Eddie Ensley, *Prayers that Heal Our Emotions,* (San Francisco: Harper-Row, 1988), p. 153.

prairie, the sun-struck desert were never out of sight and seldom more than a few dozen steps away from his camp fire. The first American was part of nature, and she of him; he knew her richness and beauty, her harshness and menace, as not one modern American in 10,000 does."[4]

Dr. Herbert Benson, author of *Your Maximum Mind* and *The Relaxation Response,* both books on right brain potential, headed up a series of well-documented research projects sponsored by Harvard Medical School to study the mind power of Tibetan monks in the Himalayas where, over many thousands of years, there have been reports of extraordinary physical and mental feats, healings, and other dramatic events.

Dr. Benson and his research crew set out on a specific project to study one particular group of Tibetan Buddhists who practiced a form of meditation called g Tum-Mo Yoga, said to allow them a right brain mind control so powerful that they could actually raise their skin temperatures dramatically in cold environments. With an indoor temperature of only 40 degrees, each monk, unclothed except for a small loincloth, sat in a cross-legged position, wrapped 49-degree, sopping wet sheets all around their bare bodies, and then began to practice their mind-altering yoga. Dr. Benson's crew watched in amazement as the monks exhibited no shivering or shaking in response to the extreme cold. Instead they sat calmly. Within three to five minutes the sheets wrapped around them began to steam. In the words of Dr. Benson: "The room filled with vapor so that the lenses on the cameras became fogged over and had to be wiped off constantly. Within 30 to 40 minutes, the sheets draped around the monks were completely dry." The monks then repeated the ceremony over a period of several hours. Not once did any of the monks show any signs of discomfort, and Dr. Benson's crew filmed and documented the entire proceeding successfully.

---

[4] Robert Clairborne, *The First Americans,* (New York: Time Life Books, 1973), pp. 22.

This incredible mind-over-matter story exemplifies the limitless spirited power of the right brain, initiated by right brain neurotransmitters which, in turn, alter electromagnetic brain wave responses. The Wu Way believes this innate spiritual nature within the human mind, once revered by ancients, has been all but bred out of the modern mind, through years of unnatural de-evolution. This innate treasure must be recalled if we are to naturalize (brain balance) our minds.

Human Brain Waves

Whether our minds are or aren't brain-balanced depends largely on the influence of brain wave response. Right and left brain behavior emanate from four different types of brain waves:

(1) Beta-brain waves are typically associated with excessive left brain output. Beta waves are the reactive brain waves emitted during most of our chaotic nine-to-five work day. In the stresses and strains of daily life, from our early morning alarm clock to our work commute and all throughout our busy day, we spend more and more time in a reactive state of mind, the highly stressed brain wave state of Beta, which is measured in cycles per second at 13 hertz.

(2) Alpha-brain waves are usually described as a catnap, daydream, or light meditative state. The highly suggestible state that hypnosis tries to cultivate is also the brain wave pattern we are in just prior to falling asleep, and again just before we fully awaken each morning. These brain waves are associated with right brain thinking and hold the key to breaking old negative patterns, as well as creating new positive ones. They are measured in cycles per second between 8 and 12 hertz.

(3) Theta-brain waves, also associated with the right brain and with a much deeper meditative or trance-like state. The g Tum-Mo Yoga described by Dr. Benson was an example of theta brain waves. This reflection of the deeper, limitless, universal mind is measured in cycles per second between 4 and 7 hertz.

(4) Delta-brain waves are associated with deep sleep. Also a reflection of right brain behavior, they are measured in cycles per second of 1 to 3 hertz.

Alpha and Theta brain wave states are prerequisite to hemispheric brain balancing which can be achieved through relaxation techniques such as meditation and Hatha Yoga. As stress mounts or expands in our daily life, we become challenged by the prospect of control loss, which triggers a primitive fear response. The fear response then motivates us to react to the problem in a left brain problem-solving fashion. This whole reflexive pattern continues throughout most of our waking day, and as stressful problems escalate, so too does the left brain's reactive mind response. More stress and more fear equal greater pressure to assert control or problem-solve, which results in more left brain output and more time spent in the stressed out/Beta brain wave state. This is exactly where twentieth-century man is today. If not for sleep, there would be almost no hope for brain balancing the de-evolved, techno-left brain, twentieth-century man.

The Unnatural Grind of the Modern Mind

As man struggled throughout history driven by his ego, the neocortex-cortex or "new brain" evolved further, developing in response to his ego's expanding needs to fulfill his corporeal desires. As he evolved in this sense, he expanded his ability to manipulate for the further attainment of his gratification via the power of violence, wealth, and knowledge, or what author Alvin Toffler refers to as the "power triad." At last, modern man has clearly established "his" world, a world reflecting the miracles created by his own hand. Yet, as he looks around he now sees many unpleasant, and indeed frightening, side effects coming back to haunt his anxious mind. Man's complex, unnatural world is at last too complicated, and his brain is simply too immersed in Beta waves for the good of his own peace of mind. His choice to impose himself on nature's design has brought about accelerated change far too difficult to cope with. As Toffler says in his book *Future Shock*, "In three short decades between now and the twenty-first century, millions of ordinary, psychologically normal people will face an abrupt collision with the future."

How did we get so far off the beaten path? Where did we come from as a species; where are we headed? It begs further psycho-spiritual inquiry. How is a mind to find any lasting peace within, amidst the thrust of such accelerated technological expansion so devoid of nature? Quite simply put, life has always been hard for the human mind to cope with, but we weren't designed to cope with what we now find ourselves up against. It is no coincidence that both our fears and our reasons for fearing are part of an expanding parallel equation. Mother Nature simply did not prepare us for such unnatural circumstances.

It is difficult enough, mentally and emotionally, for one to endure and survive the natural traumas of life beginning with his own birthing experience. "How did I get here?" "Where did I come from?" "Where am I going?" "What is an 'I'?" "What of this thing called life?" or "death?" This is all quite enough for one mind, one inner spirit to process. In fact, it remains overwhelming to most of us throughout our life process. The uneasy de-evolved modern mind is especially disadvantaged with such questions, as it becomes increasingly isolated and desensitized in the shadows of such de-evolutionary darkness. Our minds display a natural instinct to be held, loved, protected, and validated from the sting of life's earliest unresolved conflicts. Yet the reality is that all too many contemporary parents are, in fact, mere children in adult bodies, still overwhelmed, still needy, still hungry for the same love, validation, and peace of mind as their children. De-evolution has created unnecessary stresses that are above and beyond our mind's natural ability to cope.

Presently, we see endless expressions of insecure human behavior that stem from these roots, and it is remarkable to consider how far the modern, de-evolved human mind has wandered from its simpler nature.

Emotional and mental illness are currently a problem of pandemic proportions in America. According to statistics published by the National Health Education Committee, an estimated nineteen million Americans currently suffer from some form of mental and/or emotional illness. The committee points out that some emotional illness and personality disturbances are usually significant factors in criminal behavior, delinquency, suicide, narcotics addiction, and often divorce. It cites the following:

(1) 1,750,000 people are committed each year to mental institutions.

(2) 50,000 people are addicted to narcotics.

(3) 3,800,000 people are alcoholics.

(4) About 635,000 children between the ages of seven and 17 are brought to juvenile courts each year.[5]

Many of these statistics, though incredible, are conservative; they are in need of constant updating and do not really take into consideration the emotionally distraught, non-statistical, day-to-day casualty lists that grow from moment to moment. Our choice to live separated from the Wu Wei has ultimately resulted in a lifestyle filled with great mental and emotional imbalance that fails to address the need for healthy, effective coping strategies.

As we awaken each day to a world that's becoming increasingly unmanageable, we can't help but feel frightened, unsafe, and overwhelmed. We roll out of bed to the same media blitz that sings us to sleep each night; another murder in the suburbs, another drug deal in the school yard, another rape in the park. As all this mounting tension casts increasingly dark shadows on our fading sense of homeostasis, it is only natural that emotions such as fear, anger, and sadness come to the surface.

---

[5] Julias Dintenfass, *Chiropractic, A Modern Way to Health,* (New York: Pyramid Books, 1975).

As these natural emotions surface, unnatural modern man, divorced from his own inner nature, chooses to control or repress them instead of dealing with them. As these repressed emotional energies are accumulated over the course of a lifetime, they manifest as a subtle but profound pressure within, to the point where only a dynamic source of instant gratification, extending in some cases to the point of addiction, can serve to block them out. Our lifestyles have become a constantly growing source of emotional stress. Thus we are all challenged more and more by this ever-present struggle for mental and emotional balance as our de-evolved world continues to teeter on the edge between repression and addiction.

The De-Evolved Mind's Evolving Denial-Coping Systems

With so much emotion to contend with on so many levels, what's a human being to do? We have at last arrived at a point where today's most popular coping strategies include some form of desensitization and obsessive-compulsive pleasure-seeking/addiction. Alcohol, drugs, foods, sex, money, and power have all become popular de-evolutionary vehicles for short-term pain avoidance in the current scheme of human desensitization.

This desensitization process has itself become so far-reaching that it is both symptom and disease, responsible for systemic symptomatology. In truth, we are such sensitive organisms that it is unnatural for us to maintain a distance from the essence of our emotional nature for any great length of time. However, our imbalanced thinking has erroneously supported the illusory notion that we can safely and wisely choose a path of de-sensitization and denial, without consideration for either nature or our own natural emotional self. It now appears we're in a Catch-22 because we have arrived at a time in human history where all of our ego-devised systems have at last become bigger than we are. The unnatural system of life we've created in general has at last become the fatalistic monster of our own design.

In the words of the philosopher Yatri:

Violence, war, disaster, terrorism, and insanity have all become so habitual that we meet them equally with bland indifference, as though we had lost the capacity to be touched by life. We accept that it is a natural part of being human to be lonely, anxious, insecure, alienated, and in perpetual fear of death.[6]

Drugs and alcohol have become the all-too-commonplace opiates of choice in our quest to desensitize. We are so accepting of this behavior that it infiltrates nearly every area of life. Drugs and alcohol have unfortunately found their way into our daily lives from the moment we wake to the time we go to sleep. According to recent insurance statistics, driving under the influence is clearly on the increase.

A recent segment of ABC's "20/20" news program dealt with the legal indictment of a commercial airline cockpit crew accused of flying under the influence. It was reported that this particular cockpit crew of three (pilot, co-pilot, navigator) consumed seven pitchers of beer and eighteen mixed drinks among them a mere few hours before flight time. Every segment of our culture appears to be committed to desensitization at any cost with utter disregard for consequences. Alcohol has quietly become the accepted mind-altering substance that influences every aspect of our lifestyle. We drink as we drive, fly, work, or play. Strangely enough, we almost always partake in this desensitizing ritual at the most emotion-provoking times: funerals, weddings, christenings, holidays, reunions, etc. Our unnatural complex world has become far too difficult for us to cope with. What's worse, so have our natural emotional responses to it. Toffler's *Future Shock* has at last arrived, and the unnatural human mind is but one resultant casualty.

---

[6] Yatri, *Unknown Man,* (New York: Simon & Shuster, 1988), p. 16.

There is a great deal of healing yet to be gained from acknowledging our denial patterns, for our mind's systems of denial have deeper implications than most of us would care to admit. It is an issue that lies at the core of our de-evolution, and it begs for transformational healing.

In the words of sociologist-author Marilyn Ferguson:

Denial is a way of life. More accurately, it is a way of diminishing life, of making it seem more manageable. Denial is the alternative to transformation.

Personal denial, mutual denial, collective denial. Denial of facts and feelings. Denial of experience, a deliberate forgetting what we see and hear. Denial of our capacities. Politicians deny problems. Parents deny their vulnerability, teachers deny their biases, children deny their intentions. Most of all, we deny what we know in our bones.

We are caught between two different evolutionary mechanisms: denial and transformation.[7]

And it all comes down to the unnatural development or evolution of human thought and behavior. Critical incongruities result from the profound imbalance between our left and right brain development.

More and more the deductively polluted modern mind, sick from the disharmonious excessive influences of techno-industrial evolution, breeds an obsessive/compulsiveness programmed for immediate gratification. It has no time to wait for social change or transformation, nor is it able to cope with the prospect of uncontrollability, loss, pain, or the ensuing emergence of corresponding natural emotions. Therefore, denial and repression have become its counterparts. On the other hand, the simpler, uncluttered, brain-balanced pre-techno-industrial human mind reflects a more adaptive functional behavior, capable of patient, creative problem solving or

---

[7] Marilyn Ferguson, *The Aquarian Conspiracy*, (Los Angeles: Simon & Schuster, 1980), p. 74, paragraph 2.

surrender and emotional release. It is the *naturally evolved* human mind which holds the potential for transformational healing and social change.

It is clear that we have evolved, or de-evolved if you will, as a people whose imbalanced, repressive behavioral patterns sorely need the healing of natural release. Unlike the ancient Jewish cultural practice of lamenting at the Wailing Wall, or the Native American Indian tradition of embracing an oak tree for grounding as they release their grief, we avoid pain and loss through an array of unnatural denial systems. As we have evolved, we have learned well to repress our natural emotions; our unnatural minds are no longer capable of coping with them.

Human emotional repression carries a disastrous multi-generational potential. As one generation represses and denies its emotions, there is less demonstrative love, nurturance, and emotional and artistic expression passed on to the next. As the next generation displays less awareness of their emotional being, further denial and desensitization may ultimately lead to growing addiction and eventually violent, criminal, psycho-pathic (emotionally disturbed) behavior. As one disadvantaged parent from an inner-city project once told me, "Our parents were emotionally alienated, dysfunctional alcoholics. We be-came co-dependent drug addicts. And, God forbid, our chil-dren have become so psychopathically desensitized, they are now killing each other for their sneakers."

In order to heal this dysfunctional syndrome of human thought and behavior, we must rebalance our brains for the sake of our ailing minds. We must recapture the spirit of a higher order held forgotten within the brain and at last identify with the nature of our own emotional world within. This is a notion embraced by ancient natural man who was more inclined to such right brain/limbic behavior. In order for the planet to survive, we must learn to pay close attention to what we feel in our bones. We must reacquaint ourselves with natural emotion in spite of the risk of ensuing short-term pain.

We must redirect our thinking to embrace once again the natural process of life, especially at its deepest depths. For the deepest depths are where we find true emotion and conscience rather than ego. Long before the global paradigm shift, personal paradigm shifts must take root. We must rise above the de-evolutionary dysfunctional insecurity and immediate gratification/addiction syndromes to the soulful surrender, natural emotion, and higher order embraced by a balanced natural mind. It is as if dysfunctional behavior is now at its climax point in the human evolutionary spiral, like a shooting star at its dynamic peak just prior to burning out. The spirit and the soul remain the last vestige of hope for the mind's natural healing.

The unnatural mind is growing ever more reactive to this overexpansive world we've created, insatiably needy and infinitely addictive in response to the "bigger," "better," "more" ethic to which we've become enslaved. The transformational healing of the unnatural mind ultimately boils down to the struggle between ego and soul. The mind resides equally in the territory of the human ego and the soul self. Ultimately, it is the free will which determines whether we emanate from one perspective or the other. That is, one is more apt to transform toward a more natural wholeness if they are committed to following the path of the higher self. If I eat clean food, meditate, exercise, etc., then my mind/body/spirit are more apt to transform toward a greater wholeness.

We are at an important time in human history, and our minds as well as our hearts and bodies are all letting us know it. To quote Marilyn Ferguson:

We seem to be in the midst of a new Great Depression; this is not economic but psycho-social depression—the "common cold of mental health" is reportedly on the increase among pre-schoolers, teenagers, those eighteen to thirty-four, those thirty-five to forty-five, and elderly men. According to one estimate, four out of five sufferers go untreated. What does this apparent epidemic mean? And why is it happening now? [8]

Strangely enough, this wave of depression, if properly understood, may serve to usher in a new paradigm shift. As the late psychiatrist Karl Menninger once pointed out, a darkness of disturbance in the mind often precedes deep reorganization that leads to a higher norm. People become "weller than well."

I cannot help but believe that these are important times designed to raise up the phoenix of the human spirit from the current de-evolutionary tide of depression and anxiety. These symptoms, which stem from violating our natural mind, needn't result in an unending cycle of short-term pain denial and long-term suffering, but could result in the healing transformation from evolved emotional awareness.

Nature attempts to work through the ailing spirit within the human mind via the natural emanation of emotion. Nature's intention is to facilitate us with organic, emotional response as an external release in the wake of uncontrollable, mounting internal pressure. Unfortunately in the de-evolved world of today, we usually repress our emotions, which only leaves us more inclined to exhibit addictive behavior. The ancients had not yet had these emotional instincts bred out, and therefore have much to teach us.

The Emotion Within The Mind

As we learned in Chapter Three, the ancient Taoist system of "wholism" ascribed to the theory that there are five human emotions:

(1) joy
(2) anger
(3) sadness (grief)
(4) fear
(5) compassion/pensiveness

---

[8] ibid., p. 420.

Taoists taught that each of these human emotions were to be treated as varying energies that arose from all of life's possibilities, needing articulation and release. If, on the other hand, they were not fully realized and expressed, they would store in specific corresponding organs as unseen excess energy with the capability of imposing negative influence over physical health:

(1) Joy is stored in the heart.

(2) Anger is stored in the liver.

(3) Sadness is stored in the lungs.

(4) Fear is stored in the kidneys.

(5) Compassion/pensiveness are stored in the spleen.

An article written by Barbara Bialick entitled "Sounds that Heal" gives a detailed account of the Taoist teaching of the relationship between body and mind exploring how the emotions store as energies in various parts of the body, and how, through a series of yoga-like breathing, sound-releasing postures, and exercises, one can release these stored health-imbalancing energies.[9] Here again, the objective of Wu Way mind-wellness is to release and balance out these emotional energies, not store them.

Emotional pain is not to be seen as a negative but rather as an organic part of the equation—only half of a complete picture that fits together. After darkness comes the light, after pain comes the pleasure. Emotional pain needs to be understood better in our culture as part of the whole, natural picture. It has to be experienced and understood so as to be respected more as the teacher it was intended to be, rather than the prime source of human addiction and denial it has become.

The Taoists actually went to the extent of teaching that each emotion had a specific release. Emotions, it was felt, were ever-

---

[9] Barbara Bialick, "Sounds That Heal," *Whole Life Times,* (October/November 1984), p. 28.

expanding "soft-internal" formless energies naturally seeking a "denser" physical release:

Emotion	Release
Joy	Laughter
Anger	Shouting
Sadness	Crying
Fear	Groaning
Compassion/pensiveness	Song

We, too, are governed by these subtle dictates of nature. Where there is joy there must be laughter; where there is sadness there must be tears. If our ailing minds are ever to attain wellness we must first acknowledge our own natural spirit of feeling.

Summary

Currently, the human mind is tormented. Separated from nature, there is no more balance from the natural inner sensing to keep the emotions and mind clear. It is because our emotions are so repressed and misunderstood that our "false" selves emerge, ultimately banishing us to a place in the mind ruled by our dysfunctional persona. In the words of John Bradshaw, author of *Bradshaw on the Family, Healing the Shame that Binds,* and *Homecoming,* "We make culture, then culture makes us." We devise systems to serve what Jung called the persona (false self), only to find our truer self buried and victimized by the dictates of our "role self." This leads to internal conflict where self is at war with self, and self-sabotage is inevitable.

The Buddha taught that the root of all evil is ignorance and the root of all suffering is attachment to ignorance. Since the beginning of time, man has suffered as the result of his ignorance of the subtle, absolute laws of nature which ultimately demand the emergence of natural self. The ironic fail-safe here is that the suffering ultimately provides the necessary fuel to propel man through the "make/break" point of his inevitable transformation. Passed down multi-generationally, man's painful proclivity to ignore and deny have manifested as anger/grief/fear-driven "false" selves, which dualistically serve to starve from and create a hunger for the resplendent "true" self. As the Fifth Infinite Law of the Universe reminds us once again, all antagonisms are complementary, or "no pain/no gain." When we, as a culture, are at last willing to allow ourselves to feel with the tools of emotion provided by nature, only then, may we heal the endless, long-term suffering that cuts to our soul.

In order for true wellness of mind to be attained, we must first be prepared to accept this truest sense of "self." Before that can happen, we must be willing to identify with, as well as accept and forgive, both ourselves and each other as fully human, vulnerable, and real. When we can stand bare before ourselves, willing to embrace our darkness as well as our light, compassion is allowed to initiate healing unconditionally. No longer self-deprecating, self-destructive, or excessively driven, no longer addicted or incomplete, the freedom to be naturally human will at last fill the loveless void created by a desensitization born of repression from endless generations of overwhelming emotional pain. We must feel free to feel, and safe to feel, as we truly feel.

5

The Wu Way
to Mind Healing

In order to heal the de-evolved human mind, we must first take a closer look at brain wave functions. As mentioned in the previous chapter, there are four brain level states:

(1) Beta waves–stress

(2) Alpha waves–deep relaxation

(3) Theta waves–deeper meditation

(4) Delta waves–deep sleep

The Wu Way tells us the human mind has become unnatural largely due to techno-cultural maladaptations that have left it immersed in a sea of Beta waves far removed from the natural healing states of Alpha and Theta.

As our de-evolved day begins, we jump out of bed in the morning in a race against the clock. Immediately, we put on the coffee to get the caffeine into our systems to synthetically jolt our bodies into a more responsive state. Then we rush out the door to fight traffic to work, the time between often spent at work or school amidst additional competition and performance pressures. This stressful "beta" tension from modern living is ever increasing and omnipresent at work, in school, and even at home. Even mothers who once chose to remain at home in what was thought to be a relaxing, non-competitive lifestyle are now feeling new pressures to work part-time to help keep the family afloat.

And what of our relaxation time? We have been led to believe that with the new time-saving technologies such as washers and dryers, microwaves, fax machines, etc., our recreation time would increase, yet facts support the contrary.

An article in the *Boston Globe Sunday Magazine,* August 20, 1989 suggests that with the advent of all these technological time savers, we have merely acclimated ourselves to increased productivity, not more play time. In other words, we have simply created more stresses by increasing production expectations with the increased production capability. This scenario paints a worrisome picture of modern industrial-technological man racing from machine to machine, in a robotic stupor, attempting to keep abreast of hundreds of tasks and responsibilities. In comparison, for thousands of years our ancestors would engage daily in only a few focused agrarian and/or artistic manual tasks.

Currently ours is a chaotic mechanized world, and ours are beta brains, fully de-evolved due to our disordered, unnatural perceptions of life. As our disordered lives bring us stress from such unresolved chaos and confusion, we continue the beta brain spiral when we stir up highly charged overwhelming feelings and emotions until we feel incapable, unwilling, or just too unsafe to validate. Therefore, we adopt beta brain reactive defense systems of de-sensitization, repression, and addiction.

Though there is no turning back to a simpler world, the time is at hand for each of us to increase our awareness of, and adjust our behavior to, our natural emotional needs. We must ultimately embrace our pain in order to view the picture more wholistically; we must encounter the kind of change that enables our mind/body/spirit to emanate freely from within their true basic natures.

Back to Our Roots/The "Beta" Beginning

The first, and perhaps most important, step in healing the mind's emotions the Wu Way begins by identifying the roots of distorted perceptions influenced from our all-pervading, chaotic pasts. Youth and adolescent perceptions of life's conflicts and their ensuing emotions are undeveloped and often distorted. Conflict and emotion, in general, are seen by a child as "bigger than I am." As this perception becomes further internalized and reinforced throughout adolescence, its influences carry over into adulthood. This is where it becomes essential for a parent to pass the baton of self-empowerment to that adolescent. Instilling positive self-image and teaching the young adult to problem solve with self-confidence and freedom and to emote in the face of conflict are of prime importance. To modify the initial, undeveloped, defense-oriented perceptions and to reinforce the prospect that we can be "as big as" or "bigger than" our problems is an integral step in nurturing an autonomous, healthy, natural mind. If, however, that task is overlooked, the young adult is then left with the feeling of being overwhelmed in the shadow of his/her dysfunctional "bigger than I am" perception of conflict and emotion.

It is essential that each of us expand our awareness of the dynamic corollary between our human emotions and the intolerable pains resulting from disharmonious living. The Wu Way reminds us that the ultimate path of human nature leads us to a higher evolution of self, but not without pain. This painful truth which rests deeply within our emotions has a root system that holds many keys to our healing process. Confronting and releasing our often-painful true emotions frees the pressure from within that fuels the stressful mind, thus putting an end to this dis-ease process. This all-important confrontation/release process must begin by first acknowledging the roots of our pain which remain tied to our childhood and family pasts.

Without choice, we are all born into families, environments, and circumstances that are often chaotic and dysfunctional. Many of us remain victimized by repressive denial behaviors, struggling to survive physically, emotionally, and mentally. The indelible pains which result send us into adulthood as emotionally wounded children. "Co-dependent," "dysfunctional," and "adult child" are all relatively new terms that correlate these emotional wounds carried over from childhood with various denial influences. Resultant examples of this dysfunctionalism may be seen in the current trend toward ever-increasing addiction and addictive behavior. Addiction, in this sense, represents a desensitizing behavior that we may employ to repress and deny internalized emotional pain stemming from our dysfunctional family root systems. This dysfunctionalism also alludes to the shame, lack of self-esteem, and deprivation we face from an endless line of multi-generational influences.

An estimated 96 percent of the current American population has been classified as emotionally dysfunctional. The Wu Way believes that 100 percent is a more accurate estimate, an astounding figure resulting from man's choice to divorce himself from the nature to which he is inextricably bound. There are a number of successful twelve-step type programs designed to help us work through this dysfunctional behavior– ALANON (Alcoholics Anonymous), ACOA (Adult Children of Alcoholics), Child Within (Survivors of Dysfunctional Families), Co-Dependency and Dysfunctional Counseling, to name a few. There are also a number of helpful books available such as:

(1) *Recovery: A Guide for Adult Children of Alcoholics* by Gravitz and Boinder

(2) *Adult Children of Alcoholics* by Janet Geringer Woititz

(3) *Healing the Child Within* by Dr. Charles Whitfield

(4) *The Co-Dependency Series of Books* by Melody Beattie

(5) *Bradshaw on the Family; Healing the Shame that Binds You ; Homecoming,* all by John Bradshaw

Regardless of the path taken, systems of this type are designed to enable us to rebirth our real self, transcending the illusory security rendered by previously adopted destructive "false" self behavior. Truth is natural and in order for true healing to take effect, the Wu Way says we must endeavor to separate the jewel of true self from those denial masks initially created for the sake of our childhood survival.

We are born with clean slates. It is only the brush strokes of parents, teachers, friends, family, culture, and world that impressions start to form pictures. Of course, many of those impressionists are themselves tainted with dysfunctional perceptions initiated by disturbed authority figures from their own early childhood. All too many of us have grown up with parents who themselves were products of dysfunctional families. Therefore, we are left to react to the dysfunctional behavior carried over from their childhood. Physical and emotional abuse; alcohol and drug addictions; abandonment, displays of rage, fear, and anxiety were among the more blatant problems which, in turn, shaped our lives.

Ever vigilant, as insecure children we would instinctively evaluate the level of safety in our environment. If we sensed that we were unsafe, then we would adapt our behavior to compensate for our perceived lack of safety. This is what all of us have had to do as children—deny the pain, accent areas of pleasure, alter our personalities, and even become addicted to this notion of control. For a child, survival through safety is paramount. These adopted measures are lifesaving for a child too fragile and vulnerable to contend with the overwhelming sicknesses of an adult world which so profoundly affects them. Yet these life-saving pseudo-selves developed during childhood form the root system of dysfunctional adult behavior which must inevitably be replaced with "true" self. As adults, we then become responsible for this transformational discovery and emergence of "true" self. The Wu Way tells us that this healing work lies at the core of the very reason why we live and remains one of the noblest of all human tasks. Yet it comes at a great cost, for in order to initiate the work of true self emergence, we must first confront the "false" selves on which we have grown so dependent. This remains a very frightening prospect as we all continue to carry within us the spirit of a wounded child. Although the confrontation/release of our "false" selves with related emotions leaves us vulnerable at the outset, it will eventually render great strength. The Wu Way tells us that "true" self is at every moment shining within us, but because we build the protective walls of "false" selves around it, we barely see it. We must dismantle those protective walls in order that we may see the light of the soul. As an ancient Chinese proverb states, "I burned my barn to the ground; at last I can see the moon." Confrontation/release of one's pain remains the key to initiation of natural mind healing. The short-term pain arising from the confrontation of long-term suffering remains the greatest obstacle to natural mind healing.

Perhaps best put by Kahlil Gibran in *The Prophet*:

And a woman spoke, saying Tell us of Pain.

And he said:

Your pain is the breaking of the shell that encloses your understanding.

Even as the stone of the fruit must break, that its heart may stand in the sun, so must you know pain.

And could you keep your heart in wonder at the daily miracles of your life, your pain would not seem less wondrous than your joy;

And you would accept the seasons of your heart, even as you have always accepted the seasons that pass over your fields.

And you would watch with serenity through the winters of your grief.

Much of the pain is self-chosen

It is the bitter potion by which the physician within you heals your sick self.

Therefore trust the physician, and drink his remedy in silence and tranquility:

For his hand, though heavy and hard, is guided by the tender hand of the Unseen,

And the cup he brings, though it burn your lips, has been fashioned of the clay which the potter has moistened with His own sacred tears.[1]

Confronting these "selves" takes great courage as confrontation is naturally followed by emotional release. Joy, anger, sadness, fear, or compassion/pensiveness all result in a corresponding expression that is part of the release process. This process is naturally followed by a rejuvenation or healing period. All of nature moves from breakdown to transformation on a constantly changing continuum of destruction to re-creation.

Mind Healing–A Three Part Process

Healing the mind the Wu Way can be seen as a three-part process: (1) confrontation/release, (2) acceptance/forgiveness, and (3) healing/attainment. In many cases, it is essential to employ professionally trained assistance through such programs as those already mentioned. Once one has confronted and cleansed or purged oneself, it then becomes important to accept, forgive, and progress onward in the spirit of attainment.

Kenneth Pelletier, a psychologist at the University of California School of Medicine in San Francisco, is a Stress Management Specialist who echoes the sentiments of many experts in the field by feeling that:

...illness is transformative because it can cause a sudden shift in values, an awakening. If we have been keeping secrets from ourselves, unexamined conflicts, suppressed yearnings–illness may force them into awareness.[2]

---

[1] Kahlil Gibran, *The Prophet*, (New York: Alfred A. Knopf, Inc., 1923), pp. 52-53.

[2] Marilyn Ferguson, *Aquarian Conspiracy*, (New York: J.P. Tarcher, 1987), p. 257.

This shows how perfectly Nature's system works. We first violate Nature and in the process deny our own basic, true nature, thus creating pain. The pain then continues to expand in our lives until, at last, either we react and thus release it, or it seeks its own release through dis-ease/disease. At any rate, as we no longer have the capacity to store the pain, we are then naturally provided with the impetus to release it. Once released, we are then free to let go of the experience through acceptance and forgiveness, and ultimately move on to transformational healing/attainment.

Not unlike the body, the mind must first detoxify the stored emotional toxins in order to finally be rejuvenated. The rejuvenation part, or what the Twelve-Steppers like to call "Genesis," is where spiritual support, prayer, and meditation become essential. A supportive balance is more easily attained when both cleansing and healing work hand in hand simultaneously, as is demonstrated in the Wu Way's three-part process to mind healing, which includes a variety of both cognitive and behavioral techniques.

(1) **Confrontation/Release** or Rebirthing/"Natural Self-Emergence"

To gain greater understanding of the specific repressed emotional energies living within each of us: joy, anger, sadness, fear, and compassion/pensiveness, and the dynamics of how each one has affected the quality of our lives in terms of adopted behavioral patterns, awareness must be coupled with therapeutic release. As already mentioned, expression, or surrendering of these emotions in a supportive "therapy" environment is essential. "co-dependency"- "child within"- "twelve-step"-type seminars and cognitive therapy formats are most helpful in this work. Cognitive association is a successful method where a trained therapist helps the subject remember previously denied traumas and conflicts through the use of dreams, regression, hypnosis, etc. Then, with proper facilitation emotional release is encouraged in a safe environment.

The key to Wu Way mind healing at this stage calls for "clearing" repressed emotional toxicity. In any case, once the detoxification has lessened the built-up, stored emotional pressure, we are then free to feel who we are, as we are.

When working out old internalized conflicts, we do not always have the benefit of addressing those with whom we were/are in conflict. Time passes, life's circumstances change, and people die; yet unresolved conflicts remain forever etched in our minds. A lifetime of repressed anger for a father who may no longer be alive still needs release. Play-acting therapy is a very useful active visualization tool capable of helping one gain access to such sensitive issues of harbored conflict. In this kind of active, more physical visualization, one can change the memory of the past with all its related emotion. Whether the emotion is joy, anger, sadness, fear, or compassion/pensiveness, this play-acting technique affords us the opportunity to clear out old internalized repressions and the neurotic behavioral patterns that stem from them. It is suggested that a trained therapist help facilitate this exercise as there may be resulting excessive toxic emotional shock.

The Wu Way Play-Acting Exercise*
*This technique requires the assistance of a well-trained, supportive facilitator/therapist/counselor.

The play-acting technique is a form of behavior modification that enables us to change old disharmonious thought patterns by releasing trapped emotional energy. This natural mind healing method seeks to free up emotional energy stored within the body via the mind. The root of many emotional disharmonies stem from deep reactions to highly charged perceptions. Furthermore, the Wu Way, not unlike the ancient Taoists, believes that as we repress or fail to release emotional energy, we store the pure energy derived from these emotions deep within various parts of the body, such as muscles, vital glands, and organs. Therefore, release exercises such as this play-acting technique enable us to cathartically free up these emotional energies which, in turn, enables us to neutralize many related physical symptoms.

The Wu Way Play-acting Exercise is quite simple. We should first replicate or simulate the Wu Way Guided Visualization technique (detailed later in this chapter), taking the initiative to provide ourselves with a quiet uninterrupted environment. This is to be a very private, intimate, quality time! Just as with the Wu Way Guided Visualization and (following) Meditation procedures, both comfortable, loose-fitting clothing as well as consistent time and place are of great importance. Once we are assured of quiet and solitude, we are then ready to search our memory for a core conflict from the past.

To focus more clearly on this memory we may use certain audio or visual aids; a picture in our mind's eye of certain clothing we may have worn at the time, an event such as a holiday, a specific place, a time of year, or perhaps a song. We may again return to those places or play those songs to aid our spirit in accessing and thawing the frozen emotions.

Once in touch with the memory of the people and events, we may then rewrite the script and re-enact our part with the emotional response our natural self would prefer in the safety of the present. We may have a need to express repressed anger to a parent who overpowered, controlled, or abused us years ago. We are now safe to assert a firm non-abusive dialogue, thawing that anger in a healthy fashion. In Play-acting Therapy we must be willing to throw off all inhibitions and thus fully engage our body with our mind in a physical/emotional catharsis. Emotions speak through the body. Therefore, let those feelings spontaneously dictate the movement of your body during this therapy.

The Wu Way Creative Mind/Body Release Exercise
Similar to the Play-acting Exercise, this procedure helps us to release those emotional repressions that remain both trapped in the psyche and manifested in the body. This voluntary mind/body exercise is a most effective natural technique. We

must keep in mind that nature seeks to release these repressed emotions involuntarily through the body in the form of physical symptoms, designed to attract our attention back to the unattended emotional origins of the pain. Therefore, the uninhibited improvisational movement/release of body energy, coupled with the triggering of emotional release via specifically selected cathartic music, liberates repressed emotional Chi (energy) from both mind and body.

First, begin with only two or three emotions at a time. For example, you may start with joy, anger, and/or sadness. Then, listen to an array of music, making note of only those songs or compositions that specifically stimulate you through the emotions listed above. Try to assemble at least thirty minutes of music for each emotional category. Once catalogued, you may place them in any order desired, recording them onto audio tapes to be played back during the exercise. For example:

Joy: Mozart's "Horn Concerto #1 in D Major", Beethoven's "Ode to Joy"–Ninth Symphony, etc.

Anger: The Who's–"We're Not Going To Take It!", "We Won't Get Fooled Again!", etc.

Sadness: Henry Mancini's "Moon River," Dolly Parton's "Me and Little Andy," etc.

Once your songs are sequenced and taped, you must then prepare your environment, just as with the Play-acting Exercise, ensuring uninterrupted quiet and loose-fitting, comfortable clothing. Now you are ready to play your cued up selections and commence with the exercise.

Once the music begins, you may then move about in improvisational dance-like fashion inspired by the music. It is essential that you move freely without any inhibition–laughing, cheering, moaning, groaning, crying, screaming, and yelling as you so feel. Remember that this is intended to be a spontaneous release of feelings expression and sounds, passing through the body, triggered by repressed highly charged emotions. It is important not to exceed one 30-minute session per day, and to focus on only one emotion each session. Better still, focus on whatever emotion seems to need the most attention. If you are in touch with your feelings you can generally sense at least one emotion predominating at any given time. It is also likely that you will find the need to work with the emotions thematically, that is, to focus on one emotion for several sessions in succession.

Use of both the Wu Way Play-acting and Creative Mind/Body Release exercises gives us clearance to transition naturally from confrontation/release into acceptance/forgiveness.

(2) **Acceptance/Forgiveness**

This is where the rebuilding process begins after the emotional detoxification has cleared out enough space. With a new beginning, a healthier, truer self is encouraged to surface, and a secure, centered self can better accept and move beyond what went before. Old patterns, now broken, may be replaced with more healthy, well-boundaried, spontaneous behavior. There will be more action, less re-action; more natural feeling, less repression. Behavior will now resonate more consistently from the higher mind, with a greater harmony between the left and right brain centers.

The Wu Way believes this to be an area of specific importance. Many of today's clinical and behavioral counseling techniques, though helpful in the areas of confrontation/release, may in fact be considered unnatural therapies as they lack proper acceptance/forgiveness facilitation skills. Most of them take us through an endless painful rehashing of old core emotional conflicts without resolution. Many of these techniques lead us back to those painful memories with the sole intention of encouraging repeated release of highly charged feelings. This leaves us only partially cleansed, creating a need or dependency to return for help again and again. True resolution resides within the unrealized spiritual self. Proper facilitation helps us to release the healing spirit from deep within, inspiring us beyond confrontation/release, through acceptance and forgiveness to healing/attainment. Any healing system that espouses wholism knows full well the importance of body, mind, and spirit unification, as well as self-reliance. In order to truly heal the unnatural human mind, we must first seek to both unify and appeal to the separate needs of body, mind, and spirit. The Wu Way feels unquestionably that one of the core issues destroying the natural mind is the de-evolved, spiritually devoid, godless manner in which we live. Godlessness is both a cause and effect of this de-evolutionary spiral. If we are to truly heal the unnatural mind, confrontation/release of repressed emotions must be followed by acceptance/forgiveness healing through proper psycho-spiritual growth and support.

(3) **Healing/Attainment**

The final step in this process is often referred to as Genesis, where one moves beyond the old dysfunctional self toward the higher self. A new functional spiritual foundation must be established here to replace the old "worldly" standard.

Some of the tools one may use in this all-important healing/attainment process include:

(a) Visualization—To replace old, unhealthy mind programs with new, positive pictures. This solidifies or reinforces new healing mental images.

(b) Meditation—To encourage more stress-free alpha and theta brain output and to balance brain centers.

(c) Spiritual Perception Modification—To help one sense his way back to a more natural behavioral balance through both psychological and spiritual (psycho-spiritual) means, encouraging the individual toward a radical paradigm shift in perception of body, mind, and spirit back to Nature/God. Assistance of a trained counselor may be helpful, especially one with a psycho-spiritual background (psychological/theological training).

(d) Contemplation/Prayer–To affirm one's role in the ordered universe; tied to, stemming from, and revolving around an infinite force.

To expand further on these Wu Way Mind Healing techniques, we will now discuss the first three tools: visualization, meditation, and spiritual perception modification for Healing/Attainment.[3] To utilize the following visualization and meditation techniques effectively, the Wu Way recommends that they be recorded onto audio tape. They are intended to be read/recorded, as they appear, in advance, so that the subject is free to submit fully to the exercise.

Wu Way Guided Visualization–Adapted from classic Hatha Yoga Savasna technique (Active Visualization).

This visualization, referred to as active, demands a more creative imagination response. It is advised that you begin this exercise by first consulting with the meditation recommendations. However, unlike the meditation procedure, you may lie down on a comfortable carpeted floor if you so desire. If you choose to lie down, the best posture would be flat on your back, no pillow, legs shoulder-width apart, palms facing up, with hands opened slightly away from the body. You might consult a Hatha Yoga book for a posture called Savasna. This describes graphically the recommended supine posture. Once you are in position and comfortable, you are ready for the Wu Way Guided Visualization.

(Start recording here)

With eyes closed, relax and take a clearing breath, empty your lungs...then inhale, filling the lungs to full capacity and hold (3 seconds) and release fully. Now repeat a second time, fill the lungs to capacity and hold (3 seconds) and release fully. Repeat a third and final time, fill the lungs to full capacity and hold (3 seconds)...now release fully, resuming normal relaxed breathing.

---

[3] This will be covered in Chapter Six.

Focus your mind's eye on a picture of your legs and feet. Concentrate...continue concentrating on a picture of your legs and feet in your inner mind (25 seconds). Now raise up your legs and feet approximately 6-10 inches off the ground. Tense all the muscles in the legs and feet as if you were collecting all the tension stored there. Continue to tense the muscles, more, more. Take a deep breath. Hold the tension with the breath, more, more. At the count of three, you will let go of the tension and the breath at the same time. Counting One...Two...Three! Relax and resume normal breathing (20 seconds).

Now focus your mind's eye on a picture of your shoulders, arms, and hands. Concentrate...continue to concentrate on the picture of your shoulders, arms, and hands (20 seconds). Now slowly raise up your arms and hands approximately 6-10 inches off the ground. Tense the shoulders, arms and hands as if you were collecting all the tension stored there. Continue to tense the muscles, more, more, more. Take a deep breath, hold the tension with the breath, hold, hold, hold. At the count of three, you will let go of the tension and the breath at the same instant. Counting One...Two...Three! Relax and resume normal breathing (20 seconds).

Next focus your mind's eye on a picture of your chest, back, abdomen, pelvis, and buttocks. Concentrate...continue to concentrate on a picture of your chest, back, abdomen, pelvis, and buttocks (20 seconds). Now slowly tense up all the muscles in your chest, back, abdomen, pelvis, and buttocks as if you were collecting all the tension stored there. Continue to tense all those muscles, more, more, more. Take a deep breath, hold the tension with the breath, more, more, more. At the count of three, you will let go of the tension and the breath at the same instant. Counting One...Two...Three! Relax and resume normal breathing (20 seconds).

Finally, focus in your mind's eye on a picture of your face, head and neck. Concentrate...continue to concentrate on a picture of your face, head, and neck (20 seconds). Now slowly

163

tense up all the muscles in your face, head, and neck as if you were collecting all the tension stored there. Continue to tense all the muscles, more, more, more. Take a deep, deep breath, hold the tension with the breath, more, more, more. At the count of three you will let go of the tension and the breath at the same instant. Counting One...Two...Three! Relax and resume normal breathing (2-3 minutes).

Now picture in your mind's eye that you are lying on a soft, puffy cloud, slowly rolling along...Slowly you reach your legs over the edge of the cloud and like a feather, you gently float to Earth. As you softly land, the first thing you notice is high, green summer grass that gently blankets your feet...Next you notice the beauty of nature all around you...Warm blue skies, lavish green trees blowing in the soft summer breezes, birds singing, and a crystal clear lake beside you...Nothing but nature surrounds you, as if you were all alone in the garden of Eden, in a state of blissful, healing peace...You can actually feel a radiant, healing energy coming from all the nature around you...You feel a profound healing coming from the pure, natural sunlight, the breezes, the whispering pines, the dancing leaves, the singing birds. It is like nothing you have ever known before or ever thought possible...Now simply take some time to enjoy where you are. Take the time to play there, absorb the peace and profound healing (10 minutes).

By now you feel completely rejuvenated, healed by the force of nature like never before...Now that you have absorbed all of nature's healing vibrations, you are going to carry them with you for the rest of your life, only adding to the collection each time you return to your special healing place...With that in mind you will slowly float back up to your transport cloud. By the count of three you will be on board. Counting One...Two...Three, you are now back on your cloud, on your way home...The ride home will not take long (2 minutes).

Now, you will once again place your feet over the edge of the cloud and slowly float safely back to Earth where you will gradually awaken to your body awareness. There is no rush coming out of the exercise. Feel your arms and legs filled with relaxed balanced energy. Move them from side to side. Slowly open your eyes and adjust to the light. No sudden movements, no rushing about to answer phones. Allow yourself a few additional moments to carry the principal feeling into your daily life.

(Stop recording here)

Meditation

In his book, *TM, Discovering Inner Energy and Overcoming Stress*, published by Dell Books, Harold Bloomfield, M.D. searched extensively into all available scientific studies for the physiological and clinical effects of meditation, especially Transcendental Meditation (TM), and presented the evidence to the general reader in an interesting and easy-to-read format.

Dr. Bloomfield is Director of Psychiatry at the Institute of Psychophysiology Medicine at Del Mar, California. He is author of *The Holistic Way to Health and Happiness*, published by Simon & Schuster. Here is what he found:

(1) Meditation represents an exceptional state of deep rest, deeper than sleep, yet accompanied by alertness. Like the "rest" recommended by doctors to aid recovery from an illness, the TM technique gives the body an opportunity to restore energy and heal itself.

(2) Meditation lowers the body metabolism and reduces oxygen usage by 20 percent, yet produces no breathing abnormality. During meditation, subjects show a rapid reduction in nervous tension and a state of very deep relaxation. There is also a very significant decrease in blood lactic acid, the stress-related chemical. This data is from the work of Drs. Benson and Wallace.

(3) Drs. Paul Corey, Wilson, and Honesburger found that the bronchial airways opened up by 20 percent more during the practice of TM. Airway resistance improves and clinical improvements were confirmed by their own

physicians in the asthmatics studied. This suggests that the TM technique may have therapeutic application for asthma, emphysema, and chronic bronchitis patients.

(4) TM was found to be very useful in relieving insomnia, helping the person to begin an improved sleep pattern. TM can also help those who sleep excessively but awaken unrefreshed.

(5) Other conditions reportedly improved by TM include duodenal ulcers, epileptic seizures, rheumatoid arthritis, severe tension headaches, angina pectoris, and allergic conditions.[4]

Meditation, whether it be TM, the simple methods previously outlined, or any one of a number of various other methods, is an effective means of helping one to cope with and process emotional stress. It represents a healing of the spirit mind after the purging of the emotional heart. The reference to Alpha and Theta brain waves mentioned frequently in this book suggests a state of mind that is balanced, not just figuratively but in relation to right- and left-brain output. Meditation and such related relaxation therapies as Hatha Yoga, Silva mind control, and many "soft" martial art forms, have a brain-balancing effect. The hot, impulsive, addictive mid-brain output slows down considerably.

During the 1970s, Dr. Herbert Benson, a respected cardiologist from Harvard Medical School, had been studying experienced practitioners of transcendental meditation (TM). He found that once they eased into their meditative states, certain individuals could lower their breathing rate, pulse, and blood pressure at will. Benson tried to explain the process from a scientific perspective. After years of study he managed to demystify the TM process and to reduce it to a simple procedure. By repeating the same sound (OM) to oneself over and over

---

[4] Lawrence Young, M.D., Reports of the National Clearinghouse for Meditation Relaxation and Related Therapies, Vol.#1, (New York: 1980).

again in a quiet setting, an individual could produce the TM effects.[5]

Though many forms of meditation have been written about, studied and practiced, it is quite clear that alpha relaxation and all of its positive effects can be easily attained, as Dr. Benson found, in a simple procedure of single-minded exercise. To meditate effectively you should:

Wear comfortable loose-fitting clothing.

Eliminate all distraction. No television, no radio, unplug the telephone, lock the door and put out a "Do Not Disturb" sign. Make it clear that you are not to be interrupted. This is *your* time.

Sit erect with good posture, feet on the floor, spine straight, palms on lap, head erect, and facing forward, eyes closed.

Take three deep, slow breaths, then simply choose a single word to repeat in your mind. The single word you select should support your objective. Good examples are words like, "Peace," "Serenity," "Love," "God," etc.

In your mind simply repeat the word you chose over and over. Some find it helpful to use the mind's eye to picture the word on a blackboard as you repeat it. Continue this for approximately fifteen to twenty minutes. Do not focus on distractions. There is no need to chase them; they will come and go. Pay them no mind; they will diminish as your practice continues to develop the mind's concentration capability.

After approximately twenty minutes have passed (do not time yourself), slowly reacclimate yourself. Stretch out your arms and legs; slowly open your eyes to readjust to the light.

Some additional thoughts of minor importance—it is desirable to choose the same place every day if possible and to plan

---

[5] Dr. Steven Locke, M.D., *The Healer Within,* (New York: New American Library, 1986), p. 7.

an A.M./P.M. interval when possible. An example is to set up a meditation schedule for 7:00 A.M. and again at 5:30 P.M. Each session should consist of a twenty-minute meditation period.

Of all the meditation methods available, the Wu Way recommends visual meditations and visualization-type exercises. These methods employ the deep, innermost creativity of the mind's eye. They supplement deep relaxation with positive healing suggestions in the most fertile part of the mind. These guided imaginary tours are most enjoyable in that they replace meditative dogma and banality with a certain degree of creative freedom.

Once you are in the proper context, you may record the following additional meditation. It differs slightly from the "Guided Visualization", as it is self-guided, and therefore requires less creative imaginative response.

Wu Way Healing Visual Meditation (Passive Visualization)
(Start recording here)

With eyes closed and fully relaxed, I will begin by first focusing my attention on my breathing. I am fully aware of my body as I draw in air... as I release... my body parts each receive new life with each incoming breath and release any tension as I exhale. As I continue, my body becomes more and more relaxed. My body parts that might need additional relaxation will now be brought to awareness...I will release the tension in a deep breath. My feet and legs will come into attention...I will collect any tension there, take a deep breath, hold the breath for a few seconds and...release. As I exhale, I release all tension there. I will now focus on my hands and arms...I will collect any tension there, take a deep breath, hold the breath for a few seconds and...release. As I release the breath, I release all the tension there. I will now focus on my mid-section, my chest, abdomen and pelvis...I will collect any tension there, take a deep breath, hold the breath for a few seconds and...release. As I release the breath I release any tension there. I will now focus on my face, head, neck, and shoulders...I will collect any tension there, take a deep breath and hold it for a few seconds and... release. As I release the breath I will release any tension there.

Now I will just allow my entire body to relax. As I do, I now envision myself receiving a warm shower of healing, white, radiant light warming the top of my head, penetrating me and cleansing any impurities in my emotions and my mind. This healing light with all of its warmth and radiance is pouring down on and through me, washing away any and all emotional or mental toxicity, bringing healing to all areas of my mind. I will now take the time to relax and bathe in this healing light, and as I do, I will receive further cleansing and healing for my mind's thoughts and emotions, as this relaxed natural state of mind takes over my body (approximately 10-15 minutes).

Now, slowly I move away from the light with the awareness that I may return at any time to my special place. As I see the light slowly vanish, I come back to the awareness of my body, feeling relaxed and renewed, healed with my mind. Slowly I move my feet and hands from side to side. Keeping my eyes closed I become aware of where I am (10 seconds). I may now cover my eyes with my hands, so that I may slowly open them to the light. Soon I resume my normal life, but with a more natural relaxed state of mind. I will carry this mind healing into my daily life with me, and I will reinforce its presence in my life with each meditation.

(Stop recording here)

Both visualization and meditation provide means to quiet the Beta brain wave patterns and convert them into Alpha. As our world continues to de-evolve from nature and the natural mind, the Wu Way believes strongly that these techniques must become a part of our everyday lives, and that they are, in fact, becoming essential to our mind's survival.

Spiritual Perception Modification

Other embellishing aids for our perception modification enhancement might include esoteric healing, spiritual, and artistic expressions, such as the appreciation and study of

Hatha Yoga, martial arts, Zen philosophy, spiritual scriptures, art, dance, and music. These all represent spatial influences to help balance out rigid sequential thinking and thus alter unnatural, dysfunctional, temporal-mindedness.

Our unnatural mind manifests as an obsessive/compulsive, overactive, outer mind, culturally programmed and reinforced to deny both the unrealized true inner mind and the resultant emotional pain. Constantly driven to maintain its complex system of delusions and "false" selves, the unnatural mind is a controlling, repressive/addictive mind in need of profound healing. As we train our mind to let go with the help of these techniques, we find our way to a more spiritual inner life force that resonates at a more natural, peaceful pace.

It is the intention of the Wu Way that we employ this three-part system to balance both the spatial and sequential mind. This creates a greater awareness of the outer-minded "false" selves while liberating the inner-minded "true" self. To heal the unnatural mind, we must confront these "false selves" with the ultimate intention of giving birth to the natural mind within our one "true self."

6

The Unnatural Human Spirit

Even before beginning any discussion as arcane as "the unnatural human spirit" in a world as empirically reduced as ours, we should first establish some references for the term "spirit." *Webster's Collegiate Dictionary, 9th Edition* defines spirit as: "The breath of life; or the life principle conceived as a kind of breath or vapor animating the body, or, in man mediating between body and soul." Webster describes soul as, "An entity conceived as the essence, substance, animating principle, or activating cause of life, or of the individual life, especially of life manifested in psychical (pertaining to the mind) activities; the vehicle of individual existence, separate in nature from the body and usually held to be separable in existence." By now it is surely clear that we're up to our necks in esotericism, and that is exactly where the Wu Way suggests we need to be.

Currently, ours is a world dominated by sequential exoteric materialism, leaving us with little reference language, interest, and/or skill in our dealings with the topic of spirituality. This in itself, according to the Wu Way, points to a gross cultural imbalance that subtly, but profoundly, contributes to a spiritual lack of wellness in its subscribers. The Wu Way believes this ignorance, or lack of awareness, represents both cause and effect in the current dilemma of human spiritual imbalance or what is called the vice of the unnatural human spirit.

Keep in mind that the Wu Way sees balance as the optimal manifestation of wellness. Too much expansion requires a greater tendency toward contraction, and vice versa. We are a culture that has espoused excessive material and technological expansionism—bigger, better, more; power, money, sex, muscles, progress. At the same time our spiritual awareness has diminished or contracted markedly.

The Wu Way tells us it is natural for the human spirit to expand and that our failure to do so represents de-evolutionary sickness. If we choose to heal this sickness, we must first endeavor to encourage more expansive spiritual thought or awareness, seeking to live in balance between our spiritual and earthly spheres more harmoniously. Once balanced, we are then receptive to developing creative references and languages to further facilitate this new awareness.

The Wu Way reminds us that there are many pre-existing models of such human exotericism, derived from other cultures, that may help us to gain a more imaginative understanding of human spirit. For example, if we research Taoism, Hinduism, the American Indian culture, early Christianity, etc., we find marvelously imaginative, sensitive, highly developed beliefs related to spirit and soul. One can easily see these belief systems clearly embracing a deeper reverence for life than that which is materially visible and scientifically believable. These systems, less dominated by cultural exoteric materialism, display an inherent appreciation for the unseen "life force" within the life (See Chapter 3–The Anatomy of a Human Force Field).

As already implied, the Wu Way believes that we in the modern technological West have become spiritually unhealthy, simply because we have become spiritually disinclined, the result of our left-brain dominance. Here, the left brain represents ego; the right brain, soul and/or spirit; the goal being to balance the two. We clearly live in a world that has become spiritually ill because it has chosen ego over soul, greed over cooperation, anger over compassion, separatism over interconnectedness, science over religion. Ours has become a spiritually de-evolved world where the human ego has become our choice over our souls, because it alone provides us with instant gratification, and in this world of pain no one is prepared to wait to feel better. "God takes too long, and He's too unavailable." The Buddhists tell us that spiritually we have to choose between long-term suffering and short-term pain. The Wu Way agrees and reminds us that the only thing lasting about instant gratification is that it perpetuates long-term suffering. To choose the path of the ego eases the short-term pain, but furthers the long-term suffering.

The path of the soul, or God/Nature, is a path that shares the responsibility for life with all of life. We are teammates with all that lives. We are supported by it, even as we render support. We are in harmony with nature, at one in trust with God, if you will. Trust, or faith, is vital here, because natural man must use the tool of faith as his key to trust in the way of God, or the natural way, especially when things go wrong in his life, and pain tempts him to rebel against the dictates of nature. Nature, or God, is absolute and is always perfect. Even when it does not meet our ego's immediate demands, it tests our faith short-term, while yielding the natural results long-term. All we need do is either learn to exercise a spiritual trust with our inner feelings in those things we cannot see or develop our spiritual sense perception. Ancient, less de-evolved man, with his lack of technological sophistication, was more compelled to the laws of nature, and to the presence of spirit with which to perceive and resonate with God/Nature.

Throughout all human history, we see numerous examples of awe and reverence displayed by primitive cultures toward "the great unseen forces" or spiritual mysteries interwoven throughout all of life. We see an instinctive, natural need in mankind to relate to the spiritual, mystical, and mythological intangibility that surrounded him. This willingness to take esoteric risks represented a natural spiritual balance which harmonized with his exoteric, earthly inclination to work as a farmer, mason, fisherman, etc.

The ancient Greeks had an array of mythological gods that reflected their natural creative yearning to interrelate with "that which was greater." Zeus, Apollo, Aphrodite, Dionysus, Athena, Poseidon, Hera, Hestia, Ares, Hephaestus, Demeter, Hades, and Hermes all mirror the limitless depths of the unseen human condition.[1] The ancient Romans related their mythological gods to various earthly spirit manifestations. "There was Vesta of the hearth fire, Neptunus of the life-giving rain and spring water, Terminus of the boundary stone, Consus the storer, and many, many more."[2] "The ancient Vikings had one-eyed Odin and Thor, the thunder god, Tyr, Frey and Freya, Loki the mischief-maker, and many others."[3] Throughout human history we see evidence of a need to define man's existence in terms of spirit. The Wu Way recognizes the natural human instinct to relate and be related to spiritually. The human need for proof is no greater than the human need to exercise faith; the human need to reason, no greater than the human need to intuit. God, spirit, mythology, and religion have all been interwoven throughout the fabric of the human experience. De-evolved modern man, no longer of the soul, no longer of the spirit, remains in disharmony with God/Nature. His beliefs are confused, his traditions forgotten, his imagination robbed by television, videos, and movies, as his spirit grows ever unnatural and sorely in need of healing. With a sickness in the core of his spirit, the

---

[1] Ariana Stassinopoulos and Roloff Beny, *The Gods of Greece,* (New York: Harry N. Abrams & Co., Inc., 1983), p. 14.
[2] Kerry Usher, *Heroes, Gods and Emperors from Roman Mythology,* (New York: Schocken Books, 1982), p. 4.
[3] Brian Branston, *Gods and Heroes from Viking Mythology,* (New York: Shocken Books, 1982).

ripple effect in his world has become devastating. We see a steady decline in morality, values, and personal responsibility, while at the same time a steady increase in crime, addiction, and anomic desensitization.

Modern man clearly has priorities other than spirituality. The Wu Way sees the emerging unnatural human spirit coming about as the result of a systemic de-evolutionary trend away from the dictates of nature and toward human egoism. This is reflected in our current changing values toward a greater selfishness, with emphasis on materialism and technology. The priority today is material survival. Approximately 50 percent of the world population is now made up of under-thirty-year-old pragmatists who appear, most assuredly, to feel that though prayer, meditation, and spiritual awareness sound nice, they are not going to help mortgage their homes. These are hard times, perhaps the hardest of times. The Wu Way sees us fast approaching a watershed time in history with the end of the world as we've come to know it at hand. We have run out of road on the path we have chosen. The path of ego/man/technological expansionism has come full circle. In the words of Alvin Toffler, we have arrived at our own "future shock." "Future shock is the dizzying disorientation brought on by the premature arrival of the future." He adds, "Man must search out totally new ways to anchor himself, for all the old roots—religion, nation, community, family, or profession—are now cracking under the hurricane impact of the accelerative thrust."[4]

What we see here is nothing more than the classic endless human dilemma of duality. Primitive man's natural adaptational instincts were undisturbed. He was, therefore, more spiritually bonded with his inner and outer nature. Today we have hit the apex of human ego sophistication which reflects a terminal evolutionary spiral, devoid of spirituality. This is what the Wu Way calls spiritual de-evolution.

---

[4] Alvin Toffler, *Future Shock,* (New York: Random House, 1970), p. 13.

Natural Human Spirit

Nature (God)	Instinct
Spiritual (Soul)	Faith
Interconnected (Universe)	Love

Unnatural Human Spirit

Man (Technology)	Logic
Material (Ego)	Mistrust
Separate (Isolated)	Fear

We are caught in a Catch-22, for as technology is our slayer, it remains our savior in the face of the confusion and pain it has instigated.

With technology giving us the capability for instant gratification and money, the power, why wait for God? Why bother endeavoring to understand human emotion or spirit? Now, more than at any other time in history, man has created enough means to fulfill his impulsive illusory ego quest for instant gratification, supplanting even his natural instinctual need for deeper meaning.

It is not, however, solely a matter of right-/left-brain imbalance; it is much more profound than that. We believe we no longer have the need for a natural god, or for that matter, any further understanding of our own deeper self as materialistic behavior has at last become dominant. We now live moment to moment, constantly seeking gratification and pain escape, as we avoid hovering at such emotional and spiritual depths. So long as there is another "high" waiting in the wings, we are empowered to lift ourselves, or so we think. In fact, we are like mere spiritual infants deluded by the dream of self-pacification, only to be humbled by the reality that true pacification remains impossible without having our deeper needs met.

We clearly lack the natural spiritual grounding of our ancestors. Such a lack is both cause and effect in this spiritual de-evolution.

In January 1978, *McCall's* magazine published a survey of sixty thousand readers showing an overwhelming skepticism about organized religion, even among churchgoers. A poll commissioned by Protestant and Catholic groups and released in June 1978 revealed what Gallup summarized as "a severe indictment of organized religion." Eighty-six percent of the "unchurched" and 76 percent of the churchgoers agreed that individuals should arrive at their beliefs outside organized religion. About 60 percent of the churchgoers agreed with the statemen,"Most churches have lost the real, spiritual part of religion."[5]

A Catholic theologian, Anthony Padovano, remarked at a 1976 conference on meditation:

> The religious response that has occurred in the Western world–a revolution that has made us more sensitive to the religions of the Orient–is our understanding that whatever answers there are must come from ourselves. The great turmoil in the religions is caused by the spirit.[6]

The Wu Way suggests that, in order to endure and prosper healthfully in these chaotic, demanding times, we establish a personal, spiritual faith that is functional. That is, a faith that may be exercised and practiced so as to have the power to impact our day-to-day life. Difficult as this may seem to the disinclined modern mind, it could never approach the resultant pain and struggle that will accompany a posture of continued de-evolutionary spiritual avoidance. Ironically, such a process begins by first employing our logical left brain to examine intellectually representative spiritual texts and ideologies from established ancestral spiritual paths. Each of us may be uniquely attracted to a different existing spiritual path that works for us. We may discover or rediscover some traditional dogma that inspires us, or we may simply find a form of transcendentalism that resonates naturally deep within us. At

---

[5] Marily Ferguson, *The Aquarian Conspiracy,* (Los Angeles: J.P. Tarcher, Inc., 1980), p. 368.
[6] ibid.

this point, we are now free to employ right brain thought, exploring the depths of prayer, meditation, spiritual contemplation, innermost reflection, spiritual conversation, transcendental artistic expression, and various other forms of third-dimension, experiential learning.

Due to our current human, spiritual, de-evolution dilemma, we fail to appreciate the whole-istic human potential that could result from this balancing of brain hemispheres. A mind realized in spirit *and* science, is one where God and physics complete the circle. Instead, our unbalanced, de-evolved modern minds are devoid of God, who has all but been replaced by technology. And with this one-sided replacement, we have lost our natural, alpha/omega reference point. It is natural for us to have a spiritual and moral center or reference point. When our spirit grows ill, we no longer have a place to turn but back to science/man. Yet man's humanistic plight, not unlike the denser matter from which he is made, results only in limitations; science has yet to find a way to provide true lasting healing for the human heart. The result is an unparalleled spiritual war of obsessive/compulsive ego gratification/addiction. Without this final, spiritual reference point, there is only finiteness on which to depend, a finiteness lacking in the ability to truly heal. Instead, there is only addiction to the false promise of a terminal, unfulfilling finiteness, where there is never quite enough. And so we remain, not addicted to illicit substances but what's worse, addicted to our own humanness and the human systems which continue to foster the pretentious illusion of being there for us as the final reference point.

And so, we now find ourselves standing at a spiritual crossroad. We may continue to walk the path of ego/man/technology, furthering the unnatural de-evolution of the higher human mind, or we may follow a path which seeks to integrate more natural spiritual influences of soul/God/Nature so that we may at last reharmonize the human mind with the spirit and body towards true whole-istic healing.

Contemporary Western Culture and
The Unnatural Spirit

The human spirit is repeatedly assaulted and manipulated by contemporary Western culture through its media. Violence, sex, and all forms of addiction are continually used by Hollywood and Madison Avenue as manipulative weapons which give them the power to shape our highly impressionable minds and attitudes. This, in turn, enables them continued access to our innermost psyches.

Our advanced capitalist social system has established the means by which true spiritual reality has become most unreal. "More accurately, ways have been found in our consumer oriented society to reduce spiritual hungers to emotions that can be gratified by purchasing the things being sold to us through the mass media. In the context of our new social order, we more and more are being lead to believe that our deepest spiritual needs, the sort of realities that the Bible talks about, can be met simply by buying the right consumer goods. The late Herbert Marcuse went on to explain that this commercial system has so permeated our consciousness that we are now caught up in a comfortable, attractive, pleasant form of slavery. And it is the worst kind of slavery, because freedom from it becomes nearly impossible. We would never consider rebelling against a social system that gives us what we think we want."[7]

In an old barn loft of an antique shop on Cape Cod, I recently found a number of antique advertising posters from a simpler time. The Dutch Cleanser ad caption spoke of "Chasing the Dirt Away"; pictured was a grandmotherly type that you simply could not disappoint. The Morton Salt poster depicted a small girl in a yellow raincoat with an umbrella, with the caption: "When it rains, it pours." As I looked at these precious relics I

---

[7] Tony Campolo, *Wake Up America: Answering God's Radical Call While Living in the Real World*, (New York: Zondervan Publishing House, 1991), pp. 5, 10.

could not help but think how Madison Avenue would have depicted this poster today—with typically manipulative erotic overtones and some long-legged, lithe sex symbol. The implication is clear that by purchasing their product, instant gratification of a far more extensive nature is availed to us. What's worse, our materialistic culture continues to reinforce the erroneous notion that instant gratification *is,* in fact our highest spiritual goal.

The commercial industry is cold, calculated, and motivated almost exclusively by profit. They have the overwhelming power to change our minds and spirits and thus shape the behavior of an entire generation. It is truly disconcerting to consider the de-evolved state we have arrived at in the name of such "freedom" and "progress." Do we really need studies to confirm the effects of advertising on the human mind or the effects of media's sex and violence on the spiritually de-evolving human psyche? Where is our common sense? Where is our sensitivity? Where is our reverence for Spirit? Where? We need only look to our de-evolved priorities. If we are to heal the unnatural human spirit, to become more whole-istically healthy as a people, we must begin by turning inward to our innermost being. We must allow our higher self to manifest, not only after Sunday service, but in our everyday lives as well. We must, at last, balance our "man mind" with our "spirit mind" and follow the expansive physics of science into the realm of the spiritual, surrendering the false notion of control afforded us by the strict rational view of science that we fearfully cling to.

Renowned psychologist Abraham Maslow believed that strict scientific, psychological theory had centered so much on neurotic experiences that it had missed the insights to be gained by studying the experiences of healthy people. The most intense of these, which he referred to as "peak experiences," were thought to be synonymous with "religious experiences." Maslow found that perhaps the most central force of a peak experience is the sense that the whole world is interconnected and indeed has meaning, with everything fitting together and making sense, from good to evil, from order to chaos. This peak experience consciousness is arrived at through what Maslow called "clear perception" and not through some blind faith or esoteric philosophy.

At first, Maslow thought there were simply two groups—those who had peak experiences and those who hadn't.

As his investigations continued, however, he found more and more acknowledged such influences. This gradually lead Maslow to conclude that the "non-peakers" were those who were afraid of such experiences, who denied them or turned away from them. He eventually compiled a list of characteristics of these non-peakers. They typically attempt to live in a completely rational or materialistic way. Peak experiences (religious experiences) are equated with loss or irrational behavior and should therefore be rejected. Non-peakers, likewise, manifest a desperate need for control, an obsessive-compulsive fear of emotion, an ultra-scientific mentality which denies anything that is not logical, or an extremely practical, means oriented perspective (peak experiences "earn no money, bake no bread"). Given the positive benefits (profound healing) of peak experiences, Maslow judged the non-peakers to be severely limited in personal growth and fulfillment.[8]

Spirituality is natural to the human condition. There lies within, a powerful force beyond logic that seeks to direct us. This reality was more vitally apparent to our ancestors then it is to us now. Jesus referred to the Holy Spirit as the Counsellor residing within, or as a guiding Spirit of Truth. The Wu Way simply seeks to remind us that we all have a higher spirit

---

[8] Kenneth R. Overberg, S.J., *Roots and Branches: Grounding Religion in Human Experience,* (revised edition) (Kansas City, MO: Sheed and Ward, 1991), p. 6.

within, which continually seeks to work through us toward the attainment of wholeness. This attainment of wholeness comes first through the awareness of one's beingness within the context of interconnectedness. As Pulitzer Prize winning microbiologist, pathologist, Rene Dubos, in his distinguished *So Human an Animal,* said, "Whether based on religious, philosophical, or social convictions, the feeling of significance derives from man's awareness, vague as it may be, that his whole being is related to the cosmos, to the past, to the future, and to the rest of mankind. Such a sense of universal relatedness is probably akin to religious experience."[9] It remains the supreme test of the human will whether to allow or impede this natural influence. Recent movements aside, we as a culture have rejected the notion of God, higher-self, and the true wholism of nature as synonymous. Instead, we reflect a sort of spiritual schizophrenia where we confusingly cling to an egotistical notion of a god of convenience, while rejecting the universal chaos and alienation that he allows. We accept this notion of god but not the nature of the antagonism. Therefore, that which we reject we feel compelled to conquer with our own human will.

In a recent series of television interviews entitled "The Power of Myth" between moderator Bill Moyers and world renowned sociologist Joseph Campbell, Campbell suggested that this world consists of either good or evil, in a religious sense, based on whether or not an individual or his chosen religion sides with nature. He pointed out that in many of the ancient religions, such as Buddhism or Hinduism, it is often explained that "the process of nature cannot be evil." Campbell asserted that many modern Americans have rejected this religious notion of nature revealing divinity because it might have counterproductive power in our quest to achieve dominance over nature.

---

[9] Rene Dubos *So Human an Animal,* (New York: Scribner's & Sons, 1968), p. 183.

Currently, our spiritual de-evolution is transiting far beyond the mere rejection of this notion of synonymity with nature and God. We have arrived at a time where our worship of the secular "false gods" of ego/materialism/technology has led to a mass abandonment of our natural, ancestral, spiritual traditions.

In the same interview, Bill Moyers mused:

You've seen what's happened to primitive societies that are unsettled by white men's civilization. They go to pieces, they disintegrate, they succumb to vice and disease. And isn't that the same thing that's been happening to us since our myths began to disappear? Isn't that why conservative religious folks today are calling for a return to the old time religion? I understand the yearning. In my youth I had fixed stars; they comforted me with their permanence; they gave me a known horizon; they told me that there's a loving, kind and just father out there looking down to me, ready to receive me, thinking of my concerns all the time. Now science, medicine has made a house-cleaning of belief, and I wonder what happens to children who don't have that fixed star, that known horizon, those myths to sustain them?

Joseph Campbell pointed out that myths are designed to provide life models that must be appropriate at a given time, and with all the changing times, the myths must fit accordingly. Myths have intimated man's natural expressive need to relate to God/Nature or the beyond, corresponding with the times since man's beginning. This commitment dates back to cave dwellers who were compelled to relate to the mystical unknown, as we learned through their expressions drawn on cave walls. This instinct to relate is as natural for our survival as it was for our ancestors, yet our left-brain aversion to dogma and ritual discourages us from doing so. With our weighty technological influences, we have lost this vital link which naturally sustains the human spirit. Prayer, spiritual study, and worship have all become deposed contemporary relics. These represent examples of the dogma and ritual once revered as naturally healing and sustaining elements vital to the human spirit. We now live in a time when the faith experience needs to be re-awakened in the human consciousness. Psychology and spirituality must be aligned to quench the psycho-spiritual need in such a way that we can better understand the God consciousness deep within our humanness.

The Wu Way believes our current spiritual de-evolution dilemma stems largely from the unnatural human religious portrayals of God as an omnipotent, unforgiving, punitive being, with man as his hopeless, shameful victim.

The result is that many of us have rejected the notion of God altogether assuming instead a posture of rebelliousness and atheistic materialism, while others of us appear lost somewhere between the extremes of fundamentalist, guilt-ridden, sin-based religion and vague non-committal new age humanism.

Our Vanishing Sense of Spiritual and Moral Boundaries

Many of us feel the need to adopt a more personal religious posture with "invisible religion"; some, appalled by the decline in morality, adopt a more fundamentalist stance; still others simply hang onto the mainstream religious traditions that they were raised on. All this de-evolutionary confusion in the name of modernization and progress has been costly. We seem to be spiritually wayward in a much more primal sense. We are currently bemused about basic issues of morality and high-mindedness. "When we call something immoral, we are saying that it is a kind of self-mutilation, that it represents unreason-ableness in action, that it is a violation of community, and that it is a rejection of the transcendent other god."[10]

---

[10] Anisez & Shaw, *Beyond the New Morality,* (University of Notre Dame Press, 2nd edition, 1980), p. 97

During agrarian and early industrial times we were members of the classic, close-knit European extended family. Our grandparents were seen as wise, respected progenitors, who served as the last word on issues of right and wrong. The family was an institution, and God, ritual, and religion were traditions handed down with a powerful influence over our clear-boundaried sense of values. But this scenario existed well before the technological sophistication and ego displacement that gave us permission to put grandma and grandpa in the nursing home, place the "me generation" before the family, and snub our noses at God, ritual, and religion we once so depended upon for anchoring reference points.

With our current commitments to materialism, private religion, an ever-corrupt legal system, and the deterioration of the family hierarchy, we have no moral baselines left. As a result, we see mounting examples of eroding conscience. A report published by the Department of Justice in 1982 clearly indicates that we are currently a society riddled by crime. In 1981 the number of murders reported nationally rose to 22,500, a 28 percent increase within four years. Forcible rapes totalled 81,540, an increase of 8 percent over four years. Aggravated assaults reached a total of 643,720, up 4.1 percent over that period. Total robberies reached an astounding 1,321,890; an increase of 7.6 percent over that short four-year span. In addition, nationally in 1981 there were 103,000 prostitution arrests, 487,000 drug abuse arrests, 41,000 illegal gambling arrests, 1,089,000 drunken arrests, 91,000 curfew violation arrests, and 145,000 runaway arrests.[11]

Can we honestly respond to such figures with conclusions that the human spirit is alive with conscience? Religion, dogma, and ritualism aside, how are we to contend with our all-but-deteriorated sense of right and wrong? For the human con-

---

[11] U.S. Bureau of the Census, Statistical Abstract of the USA: 1982-1983, 103d edition, (Washington, DC, 1982), pp. 171-182.

sciousness to evolve spiritually and for the development of good conscience, this is among nature's highest designs. This is the Wu Way.

The classic duality of good versus evil represents the eternal fundamental human challenge and, in the final analysis, mirrors the spirit in us all with the choices we make. The Wu Way feels strongly that we must at last consider reapproaching our ancestral, spiritual traditions and disciplines with a renewed spirit of commitment and a sense of balance in the face of our boundariless, dysfunctional, spirit de-evolution.

Summary

Natural human spirit evolution is not about perfection, guilt, or sin. Nor is it inspired by a reactionary, rebellious, humanism that feels victimized by religious models that embrace such destructive precepts. Natural human spirit evolution reflects the ultimate personal responsibilities that remain tied to the very reasons why we live. And, to grow in our deepest awarenesses and sensitivities and transform through wisdom from the darkness of fear and hatred to the light of love and forgiveness. For now, we have "lost the way." We have lost interest in seeing ourselves as part of the universal scheme. Whole-ism is not dead, for the Wu Way tells us it is innate to the human consciousness. But if it is not yet dead, it is surely asleep. If we ever needed to find our innate spiritual selves and get back to the fundamental transcendental practices of our ancestors, with their innate·understanding of unwritten spiritual law, it would have to be now.

For now, you can think of God as a higher truth, a wider reality, natural order, divine safety and love. By this I mean eternal reality that is generous and kind and loving. You can make any human image of this that you will, but once you have located your core, your shining light, you will know who God is.

The greatest war in life within each individual is between the intellect and the heart—where the heart is saying "This is so" and the intellect is saying "I don't understand, therefore I don't believe."

When your mind asks "Why?", you realize how easily it is satisfied with a superficial answer. When your heart asks "Why?" it wants nothing but the truth of God.[12]

At last, both universal nature and our own basic inner nature call to us in unceasing whispers and screams. This painful, prolific de-evolutionary void begs us to once again return home to God, Nature, and the conscience of true self.

---

[12] Pat Rodegast and Judith Stanton, *Emmanuel's Book*, (New York: Bantam Books, 1987), p. 29.

7

The Wu Way to Natural Spirit

Just what exactly is man's most natural spirit persona? Taoist Master Su-Wen once wrote, "Yin (dark)/Yang (light) is the way of heaven and earth, the fundamental principle of the myriad of things, the father and mother of change and transformation, the root of inception and destruction."[1] This fundamental principle teaches us that man, like all else, is bound by duality. Therefore, this implied affirmation of the presence of higher and lower spirit nature nullifies any philosophical conjecture over whether man's inherent spirit persona is either good or evil. Of much greater importance, we should ask instead, "Where is man's natural, spiritual destiny?" Beyond his good and evil natures, "What is his resolve?" One of the Taoist Principles of the Infinite Universe states, "That which has a front has a back." Another states, "That which has a beginning has an end." These principles, coupled with the Universal Law which reminds us that all things progress from Yang (light) to Yin (dark) and Yin to Yang in continuous pendular movement, serve to point out to us that the destiny of man's natural,

---

[1] Master Ni,Hua-Ching, *TAO: The Subtle Universal Law and the Integral Way of Life,* (Malibu, CA: The Shrine of the Eternal Tao, 1979), p. 14.

189

spiritual evolution is indeed orderly (in spite of the apparent chaos), sequential, and progressive, ever advancing him through a process of refinement from light through darkness and back to a greater light. As Taoist Master Ni,Hua-Ching also reminds us, "The *true* nature of the universe, and thus that of every human being is creative, productive, *progressive, orderly,* and *harmonious.*"[2] But the Taoists are not the only ones that feel this way about man's natural, spiritual evolution. Christian belief tells us that man is of a flawed or fallen nature as the result of his willful rebellion against his Creator. But keep in mind, Christianity also believes that man was first made in the image of God. Thus, created by the Light, intended to live in the Light, he willed himself to darkness. Therefore, his natural, eternal destiny remains to confront his worldly will (ego) and reconcile his willful error so that he may at last unify once again with the Supreme Light. The Wu Way ascribes to the belief that man, while born of a dual nature (good/evil, high spirit/ego, light/dark), has a natural spiritual destiny to progress forward, sequentially, ever advancing his consciousness toward a greater Light. This, the Wu Way tells us, is *the* way of nature, representing the most consummate manifestation of healing, for it intimates the supreme purposefulness of human existence. The healing purposefulness comes with a painful price; unseen universal force creates a great cleansing tension throughout this natural, progressive transit, out of the darkness of ego into the light of higher spirit. Again the Taoists put it quite simply, "Where there is agitation, there is complimentation." Thus, through chaos and tension there is always purification. And though our "ego comfort zone" feels personally violated when life brings this agitation, a greater order to which we belong is always being served. "The universe is a model of Supreme order, the perfection of which is beyond the ability of the mortal mind to arrange, imagine or describe. Harmony is the subtle yet inviolable power of the universe, whereas force

---

[2] ibid. p. 42.

and violence are aberrations...We need only to break through the shell of ego to realize that we are one with the universe and that our concepts of externality and separateness are simply perceptual errors."[3]

Perception

These perceptual errors of externality and separateness represent but illusions which make up the framework for the ego shell (lower nature) and consist of thoughts that emanate from a mind-set influenced by a predominantly material culture. What we've been taught to think we are, we believe we are, regardless of whether it is truth or illusion. But because cultural, material advancement has taken priority over the evolution of our individual, higher spiritual nature, we have been programmed to think we are creatures of a predominant ego nature. And, so as we have been programmed to think what we are, we are. In the words of the Buddha, "All that we are is the result of what we have thought. It is founded on our thoughts; it is made up of our thoughts." To quote Marcus Aurelius in his Meditations, "Our life is what our thoughts make it."

But the natural way of things serves as the final criterion in determining truth or consequences. The result of our material and technological programming is that we've become spiritually imprisoned by the impervious shell of ego while we remain alienated from our own natural sense of higher spirit. Again, the key word here is natural, for Nature always has the last word. Therefore, if the natural truth be told, we may be what we think we are simply because we think it, but if Nature's laws are violated in the process, a systemic disharmony that will not yield to compromise will result. In spite of our modern day, materialistic brainwashing, we must come to realize that we are not exclusively creatures of ego. Everything in nature points to the fact that we are both ego *and* higher spirit with a natural destiny to evolve. But our all-important

_____

[3] ibid. pp. 41-42.

perceptions must change first, for our de-evolved perceptions remain pivotal to our spiritual growth. Perception is everything!

A favorite story of mine, as told by author Robert Fritz in *The Path of Least Resistance,* illustrates a humorous side of this interesting dilemma.

There was a man who woke one day convinced that he was a zombie. When he told his wife he was a zombie, she tried to talk him out of his outrageous opinion.

"You are not a zombie!" she said.

"I am a zombie," he answered.

"What makes you think you are a zombie?" she asked rhetorically.

"Don't you think zombies know they are zombies?" he answered with great sincerity.

His wife realized she was not getting anywhere so she called his mother and told her what was going on. His mother tried to help.

"I am your mother, wouldn't I know if I gave birth to a zombie?"

"You didn't," he explained, "I became a zombie later."

"I didn't raise my son to be a zombie, or especially to think he's a zombie," his mother pleaded.

"Nonetheless, I am a zombie," he said, unmoved by his mother's appeal to his identity and sense of guilt.

Later that day, his wife called in their minister to talk to her husband.

"You are not a zombie. You are probably going through a mid-life crisis," the minister said, trying to be the psychologist he always wanted to be.

"Zombies don't have mid-life crises," was all the man replied.

The minister recommended a psychiatrist. The wife got an emergency appointment, and within the hour the husband was in the psychiatrist's office.

"So you think you're a zombie?" the psychiatrist asked.

"I know I'm a zombie," the man said.

"Tell me, do zombies bleed?" the psychiatrist asked.

"Of course not," said the man. "Zombies are the living dead. They don't bleed." The man was a little annoyed at the psychiatrist's patronizing question.

"Well, watch this," said the psychiatrist as he picked up a pin. He took the man's finger and made a tiny pinprick. The man looked at his finger with great amazement and said nothing for three or four minutes.

"What do you know," the man finally said. "Zombies do bleed!"

This humorous story represents a not-so-humorous reality crisis in each of our lives. We've de-evolved to the point where we live our lives alienated from our own emotional/spiritual selves. This one-dimensional material/ego mind-set needs to be surrendered in order that our repressed, higher spirits may, at last, naturally evolve. We exist within the realm of duality—good/evil, high/low, happy/sad—destined to grow and evolve emotionally and spiritually. Therefore, we must accept that we are so much more than fearful, defensive, superficial creatures of ego, bound by or restricted to a terminal or mortal material existence. We must take the risk of looking to our own conscience, to our own inner self, to our own inner values and establish more whole-istic, natural criteria for our reality base. If breaking this shell of ego does, in fact, place us on the ultimate path of our natural, intended, spiritual unfoldment, then we must ask, "How does one break this primordial shell?" The Wu Way believes it is a matter of learning how *not* to live in it!

The How "Not" To

Wu Wei, as discussed in the Preface, is literally interpreted as the path of non-action. To reiterate, it is a philosophy that reminds us that God's/Nature's force is endlessly at work, in spite of man's opposing ego, and therefore, the less that man's ego does, the more apparent becomes the work of God/Nature (natural self). The "how to" is all about surrendering the illusory (ego) self, so as to allow the higher spirit self to emerge. In essence, it is more a matter of doing less, or learning how "not" to. The Wu Way acknowledges that this work is not about spiritual perfection but rather the simple evolution of love. It's all about progressing in the spirit of love. It is all about replacing fear with love, a gradual letting-go.

As long as ego remains the predominant force in our lives, we severely limit our spiritual self and, therefore, whole-istic healing capability. For our egos support the illusion of protection and power, which keeps us from growing. In the words of Thomas Merton, "We can not find Him Who is Almighty unless we are taken entirely out of our own weakness. But we must first find out our own nothingness before we can pass beyond it: and this is impossible as long as we believe in the illusion of our own power."[4]

Not unlike Merton, the Buddha proposed that only through ego detachment could a human being attain a state of peace and wholeness. "If Jesus, the healer, taught us anything, he taught us that the way to salvation lies through vulnerability."[5] Tibetan Buddhist Master Chogyam Trungpa Rinpoche often stated that in order for us to transcend our material spirit, we had to be prepared to "strip ourselves to the veins."

The vulnerability that comes from the process of surrendering ego is what ultimately allows the door to open for God/Nature/Higher Spirit self to fill the remaining void. This is the crux of natural spirit emergence. For only when we are empty, may God/Nature/Higher Spirit self fill us full. It is natural instinct that we gravitate towards the light, but we must first let go of the armor of darkness. "For no matter how much we like

---

[4] Thomas Merton, *No Man Is An Island,* (Jovanovich, NY: Harcourt, Brace, 1983), p. 234.

[5] M. Scott Peck, *The Different Drum: Community Making and Peace,* (New York: Simon and Schuster, 1987), p. 227.

to pussy foot around it, all of us who postulate a loving God and really think about it, eventually come to a single terrifying idea: God wants us to become Himself (or Herself or Itself). We are growing *toward* godhood. God is the goal of evolution. It is God who is the source of the evolutionary force and God who is the destination. This is what we mean when we say that He is the Alpha and the Omega, the beginning and the end."[6]

God is absolute love, existing on an endless, all-encompassing, continuum unrestricted by the material limitations of time and space.

Each one of us is confronted with material limitations and therefore must be willing to surrender our fear-based ego in order to engage our higher spiritual consciousness in the pursuit of connecting with the "isness" of God.

Obstacles on the Path

This healing replacement of higher spirit for ego is no simple matter, for in our culture, from childhood, our innate higher spirit is programmed out of us. We are raised to become "civilized" in such a way that benefits not any true spiritual purpose, but rather the good of material society. Today, even as early as childhood, we are abruptly weaned off our most basic mystical nature. We see increasing evidence of this as younger and still younger children prematurely imitate and emulate adult-like materialism in our de-evolving world. It is not uncommon to see eight- and nine-year-old girls wearing make-up and tight skirts, while young boys of the same age display a macho exterior, a "Jordache look," and an MTV attitude. Our natural, mystical spirit unfoldment and our naive innocence are now shamed, denied, and all but buried. In his book *A Gradual Awakening,* Steven Levine suggests that we have a great sense of unworthiness which comes from being talked out of, trained out of, conditioned out of trusting our natural being.

---

[6] M. Scott Peck, *The Road Less Traveled*, (New York: Simon and Schuster, 1979), pp. 269-270.

The very prospect of spiritual growth/ego detachment poses a formidable challenge to anyone of this spiritually de-evolved generation. In essence, the mere notion suggests a cultural revolution in the most personal sense. Today, our materially enterprising world is built upon precepts that both require and foster a highly developed human ego persona. To embrace the process of personal spiritual emergence is to reject the very illusionary foundation of self to which we think we are anchored. For this emergence of soul-self signifies certain death of both ego-self and the tapestry of illusion to which it remains entangled. In our world, our ego personas are highly programmed, intended to serve and maintain establishment organization, control, and material productivity, while over-shadowing our "counterproductive" inner core, emotional and spiritual selves. The by-products of this inculcation remain our biggest obstacles on the path of natural higher spirit emergence. Most ancient cultures considered personal *spiritual* development to be the cornerstone of healthy *human* development. Mysticism, spiritualism, and tribal rights all reflected their natural yearning to reach out beyond themselves into the greater beyond of spirit. This veneration for "that which is greater" remained firmly at the hub of their existence. Everything they did, from their exercise of ritual to their daily tasks, revolved around this ethereal, mystical focal point.

Today our focus is purely somatic. Our lives revolve around an ego axis of worth and productivity. We have reduced ourselves to haves and have nots, doers and can't doers. Everything we are, do, and say is prefaced with a spiritually devoid form of material humanism which shows little concern for inner self, nature, or that which is greater. Ours is an ego system, a system of false pride, aggression, greed, fear, rage, and resentment. The extreme highs and lows, haves and have nots, all or nothings are by-products of a duality to which we remain enslaved. We remain terminally compelled to one extreme or the other. As haves, we are often subject to the obstacles of false pride, aggression, manipulation, greed, and fear. As have nots, we may be more inclined to rage, resentment, and aggression, which may especially be directed toward the haves. All of these things represent formidable obstacles which dam the path to our natural, higher spiritual evolution. And each of *these* obstacles is, in turn, further reinforced by the obstacles of denial and desensitization. We feel we are safe so long as we may not be held responsible for what we are not aware of, and we surely lack awareness of God/Nature/Higher Spirit self and its mystical interconnectedness.

We are continually programmed towards denial and desensitization by a world culture that has turned obsessively to various means of obtaining instant gratification from the exercise of personal power in pursuit of the false promise of "the highest high." We are taught at an early age to deny pain, to desensitize or anesthetize ourselves to physical, emotional, or spiritual vulnerability. We employ denial with the help of alcohol, drugs, food, sex, money, and personal power which, in turn, compel us to remain imprisoned within this binding cycle that remains in direct opposition to the liberating path of spiritual emergence. If we are to overcome these obstacles of denial and desensitization, or for that matter, the obstacles of false pride, aggression, greed, fear, rage, and resentment, we must first be willing to cultivate or till the soil of the higher self, so that our innermost spirit nature may blossom through.

Living in the Moment
(The "How To"– "How Not To")
The process of personal spiritual evolution does have specific application. In fact, the Wu Way believes it is essential for one to review systems and functional methodologies in order to cultivate the "how not to" mind-set.

Beyond the philosophical aspects of the "just letting go," the gradual process of overcoming our lower nature requires specific spiritual exercise. The Wu Way tells us that the secret to this business of learning how to do less in the ego and more in the higher spirit, lies in the art of learning how to "live in the moment." The past and present are cerebral dwelling places of great distraction to the higher self and, therefore, are to be seen as domains of the ego. Keep in mind here that the Wu Way acknowledges that it is perfectly natural for us to transit fully through our emotional beings, and thus experience the powerful influences of past, present, and future *on the way* to higher spiritual emergence. It is all sequential, progressing from emotion to spirit, from psycho to spiritual. We have been told that the heart knows the soul best. But, choosing to remain emotionally repressed or obsessed *stops* the progression of our higher spiritual evolution. Repressing our core emotional being blocks the ultimate natural transit to spirit, and, while dwelling in the past results in emotional depression, dwelling in the future invites chronic anxiety. Only when we remain fully conscious in the present do we remain clear enough in thought to let our higher natural spirit self surface.

We should point out here that this is no bad rap on the long-term planning skills of the cerebral cortex, spoken of earlier in this book, as these cortex planning skills are of a higher *deductive* nature, whereas this "in the moment" thinking represents an *inductive* Alpha brain wave clearing of the mind. It points to the consummate peace-rendering spiritual exercise of prayer and meditation that Eastern and Western religions alike have alluded to for centuries. The Wu Way strongly agrees here that the keys to the art of "living in the moment" remain the incorporation of daily prayer and meditation in our lives. The distracting Beta brain waves, which predominate in our hectic, stressful, ego world must first be stilled if our higher mind is to emerge. These keys, prayer and meditation, represent the tools of cultivation with which we may "till the soil" of the mind. Only when the mind is centered and undistracted may it then be fertile for the emerging growth of higher self.

Intellectualizing this process is one thing, while practicing it is quite another. In our world, the powerful Beta brain vacuum is likened to an oceanic undertow whose pull constantly tests the strength of our direction. Keep in mind that despite the fact that the world was a much simpler place with far less material distraction two thousand years ago. The Buddha implored followers of the spiritual path to "sit" (meditate) tirelessly, while Jesus counseled to "pray without ceasing." If these were the spiritual prescriptions of a much simpler place and time, what must they be today? Therefore, the Wu Way suggests we commit ourselves to consistent, unconditional practice of these disciplines for the good of our natural higher spirit emergence. In our world, the growth of spirit must at last become *the* priority if *true* whole-ism is to yield its full healing potential in our lives. And while prayer and meditation are seen by the Wu Way as key "how tos" in this process of higher spirit unfoldment, the Wu Way feels that the real key lies in our ability to live day-to-day life in a more prayerful, meditative fashion. That is, to make our living a more mindful, fully conscious experience–to affirm and cultivate a greater presence of living conscience.

Nietzsche's *Thus Spake Zarathustra,* reminds us that your very "self" must be in your action as the mother is in the child, as our formula for higher virtue. Spiritual teacher Ram Das, tells us that we must learn to "be here now!" Hindu thought likens the ego aspects of the mind to be like wild horses which need to be trained or stilled. It is only through constant meditation practice, they tell us, that this can be done. The Buddhists simply say, "When eating, just eat. When walking, just walk. When sitting, just sit." Practicing the art of living with full consciousness, focusing only on the moment at hand, ultimately opens the window to the soul. But the process of opening this window requires guidance. The Wu Way believes that before we enhance our personal, spiritual evolution with the disciplines of prayer, meditation, and "living in the moment" consciousness, we need a sense of direction and boundaries.

Spiritual Direction and Boundaries

At first this search is predominantly intellectual. That is, we must seek out, review, and analyze various spiritual traditions in hopes of finding one that we seem to naturally resonate with, so that we may find a spiritual system that provides us with a guiding framework. We may look to the existing traditions of Christianity, Judaism, Buddhism, Islam, Hinduism, Zoroastrianism, etc.; or, if we are less inclined toward dogma and/or ritual, we might prefer to examine spiritual philosophies, such as Vedanta, or transcendentalism. In any case, we need to come away with a "way," or a vehicle that provides us with the means for activating our practices, so that we may, at last, expand the emerging potential of our higher spirit self. As author William Glasser, M.D., tells us in *Take Control of Your Life,* we humans have a two-part behavioral system. One contains the inherent organized behavior, the other the reorganizing behavior. Our de-evolved culture has ill-fatedly expanded far beyond its natural inherent need for ordered, social systems and traditions in general. This is clearly in evidence with our current abhorrence for religious structures.

In the introduction of his book entitled *The Book of Macrobiotics, The Universal Way of Healing and Happiness,* Michio Kushi writes, "Religious traditions which have inspired people's conscience for many centuries have declined, and their establishments have lost their attraction for the people."[7] This, he tells us, is one of the major reasons for the degeneration of modern man. The Wu Way believes that our natural instincts require the order and traditions reflected in specific teachings, inspirations, role models, prayers, meditations, contemplations, and the like. Specifically, these traditions provide a framework that enables us to exercise our higher spirits more freely and expressively surrendered within the realm of healthy bound-

---

[7] Michio Kushi, *The Book of Macrobiotics: The Universal Way of Healing and Happiness,* (Tokyo: Japan Publishing, Inc., 1983), p. 3.

aries. Once our search has helped us to identify with a functional system, we are then ready to exercise with discipline and consistency. Discipline and consistency of practice build strength which, in turn, opens doors to the most profound element of spiritual surrender. The Buddhists refer to this as saddha, or strength born out of conviction. We might simply call it faith.

Faith

Faith remains the most vital ingredient to human spiritual evolution. It represents the ultimate soulful surrender or belief in an unseen, yet undeniable, natural order and higher power. In the words of Emerson, "There are unseen laws that execute themselves. They are out of time, out of space, not subject to circumstances. Thus in the soul of man, there is a justice..." Such trusting faith surfaces only after the realization that life's purifying pains are never healed through logic and worldliness, but through the evolution of spirit—faith results only after knowledge has exhausted itself in futility. M. Scott Peck relates in his work, *The Road Less Traveled,* "Spiritual growth is a journey out of the microcosm into an even greater macrocosm. In its early stages it is a journey of knowledge and not of faith."[8] When we can no longer find our peace in the knowledge of what we once held as true, the illusion of our false security becomes exposed. All that remains before us, then, is a vast open space. It is that open space that calls us to a "leap of faith." As author W. Phillip Keller says, "It takes courage to do this. A daring act of faith is required for us to let go of the limb to which we have clung for so long and launch ourselves fearlessly into the great open space before us."[9] This represents the fundamental spiritual challenge before each and every one of us—a challenge designed by God/Nature to purify and refine

---

[8] M. Scott Peck, *The Road Less Traveled,* (New York: Touchstone Books, 1978), p. 193.
[9] W. Phillip Keller, *Sky Edge,* (Waco, TX: Word Books, 1987).

us as spirits while at the same time serving to heal us in all other areas of "being."

Clearly there are many agnostics who will question the necessity of such wisdom. I am not certain that in a short-term microcosmic, or worldly, intellectual view there is any necessity. It appears evident only from a macrocosmic vantage point manifesting as "nature's way forgotten," inner self buried, or "paradise lost." The Wu Way teaches us that spirituality in modern life is not unlike modern medicine's interpretation of the appendix as a vestigial organ. It has been neatly stricken from our list of necessary concerns, yet in its absence from our consciousness, its natural purposefulness continues to haunt us. The Wu Way believes that God/Nature has already predetermined the framework for all appropriate living. Our lot is to apply "childlike" faith and comply harmoniously with God's/Nature's dictates, fulfilling the teaching of Christ when He taught us, "Thy will be done."

Faith must be recognized as the highest form of spiritual trust. It is a trust that far supersedes any left-brain comprehension and the ultimate living manifestation of spiritual affirmation. As the philosopher Hildegarde of Bingen once said, "Trust shows the way."[10] Meister Ekhart tells us, "You can never trust God too much. Why is it that some people do not bear fruit? It is because they have no trust either in God or in themselves."[11] Once we've spiritually evolved to the point of activating our faith, healing can then take on profound meaning.

The conviction of "living" faith is actually the most significant ingredient in any true whole-istic healing. It is living faith in absolutes (God the Father, the Tao, the unseen way of universal nature) that may be seen as the slayer of the destructive elements of the ego, or Satan. In the scheme of the universal principle of agitation/complementation, it is our

---

[10] *Original Blessing,* (Santa Fe, NM: Matthew Fox, Bear & Co., 1983), p. 81.
[11] ibid.

harmonic soul set against our discordant ego which sees itself as separate from nature, natural law, and God. For as we live in denial of these unacknowledged truths, we further ensure our own psychic/physical pain and bondage. Faith suggests surrender to those natural higher forces affirming the commitment that "Thy will," not our will, "be done." It is through the activation of faith and surrender that we accomplish what the Wu Way calls "ego detoxification." This is where we rid ourselves of the toxic effects of ego, so that we may begin the process of healing the whole self through the spirit. The power of such healing comes only as the unconditional surrender of ego self is replaced by the force of spirit. The Bible tells us of a woman who, suffering with severe uterine hemorrhaging, merely touched the hem of the garments of Jesus of Nazareth and was completely healed. Her bleeding stopped instantly, and as she turned to Jesus she praised Him for healing her. To which Jesus replied, "Daughter, your faith has healed you."[12]

Even some modern men of medical science are now questioning the importance of faith in healing.

A Viennese doctor, Dr. Hans Finsterer, who believes "the unseen hands of God" help make an operation successful, was selected by the International College of Surgeons for its highest honor, "master of surgery." He was cited for his work in abdominal surgery with the use of local anesthesia only.

Finsterer, a seventy-two-year-old professor at the University of Virginia, has performed more than 20,000 major operations, among them 8,000 gastric resections (removal of part or all of the stomach) using only local anesthesia. Finsterer said that although considerable progress has been made in medicine and surgery in the past few years "all advances are not sufficient in themselves to ensure a happy outcome in every operation. In many instances," he

---

[12] *The NIV/KJV Parallel Bible,* (Grand Rapids, MI: Zondervan, 1983).

said, "in what appeared to be simple surgical procedure the patients died, and in some cases, where the surgeon despaired of a patient, there was recovery.

Some of our colleagues attribute these things to unpredictable chance, while others are convinced that in those difficult cases their work has been aided by the unseen hand of God. Of late years, unfortunately, many patients and doctors have lost their conviction that all things depend on the providence of God.

When we are once again convinced of the importance of God's help in our activities and especially in the treatment of our patients, then true progress will have been accomplished in restoring the sick to health."[13]

In *Minding the Body, Mending the Mind*, author Joan Borysenko relates this interesting story, "A study by Dr. Yajiro Ikemi and his colleagues in Kyoto, Japan, centered on a small group of survivors from cancers usually considered incurable. The patients all told a similar story. Their reaction to the diagnosis was one of sincere gratitude for whatever life they might have remaining. They focused on the glass as half full rather than half empty. The cancer had appeared in all five patients at a time of severe existential crisis. The patients had reframed their crises as an opportunity to resolve the issues that led up to them. They were challenged by, and accepted responsibility for, their situations. Finally, all the patients completely and sincerely committed themselves to the will of God."[14] They exhibited complete and utter faith and trust in God and God's will and were all fully cured. Faith, when actualized through affirmation, prayer, or meditative focus, represents an unlimited source for healing. According to Mark 11:24, "Whatever you ask for in prayer, believe that you have

---

[13] Norman Vincent Peale, *The Power of Positive Thinking*, (New York: Random House)

[14] Joan Borysenko, Ph.D., *Minding the Body, Mending the Mind*, (Reading, MA: Addison-Wesley Pub. Co., Inc., 1987), p. 11.

received it, and it will be yours."[15] Matthew 9:29 tells us, "According to your faith will it be done to you."[16]

There is a wealth of documentation available highlighting the unparalleled healing power of faith actualized in prayer. In *The Power to Heal,* Francis MacNutt, details countless such events. For example, Lisa Scarborough was initially diagnosed at two-and-one-half years of age as having a brain tumor, but in fact, was finally and correctly diagnosed as having a demyelinization of the nervous system, or Multiple Sclerosis. The author tells how Lisa progressively lost her sight, speech, and general muscle coordination, only to be totally restricted to tube feeding and confined to her hospital bed. Her spine had such a curvature that her rib cage protruded causing total body deformity. From April 22 through April 29, 1976, Lisa received what is referred to as "soaking prayer."

Soaking prayer is a technique whereby a small group of faithful gather together over the subject in prayer for approximately ten minutes—a visualized common goal is feverishly prayed for and, with the utmost of believing faith, expected to be granted. During that one week period it was witnessed and documented that Lisa's spine straightened completely, and for the first time in her life she was able to lie on her stomach. It was also noted that her neck had gained considerable mobility, and her once severely protruded left rib cage was markedly decreased.

MacNutt, in what he calls "the most remarkable example of healing through soaking prayer I ever saw," tells the incredible story of one Teresa Patino. Teresa's healing experience took place in Sanson-Rionegro, Colombia, South America, in February 1975. A team of eight people, including a bishop, two priests and one nun, performed a prayer soaking over nineteen-year-old Teresa, who was medically diagnosed as having a severe case of osteomyelitis, which resulted from stepping on a sharp

---

[15] *The Parallel Bible,* p. 1261.
[16] *The Parallel Bible,* p. 1210.

object in a swamp when she was only five years old. Her right leg, severely warped from the knee down, was approximately six inches shorter than her left leg. She also had a deep scar where an unsuccessful bone graft had been attempted.

After only two hours of gentle prayer soaking, the leg grew one inch. The same results came with a second session later that day. Again the leg grew one more inch. Two more hours the following morning produced the same results—another inch. By the end of the second day and after the fourth prayer soaking session, her leg had extended nearly four inches. In the worlds of MacNutt, "Most remarkably, though, the right foot, which was flat and had no arch to speak of, grew and changed shape until the arch came in as in the normal foot. The toes on the other foot also grew until they were almost the size of those on her normal foot. In a period of hours, her toes on the right foot had nearly doubled in size."[17]

By the fourth day two medical doctors confirmed that her bone had completely welded and her leg had grown to near full extension. Free from all pain and discomfort, Teresa walked for the first time in fourteen years. The human spirit represents the untapped limitless human potential of the higher mind focused in the most noble of directions, unrestricted by ego or logic, actualized by exercised affirmations of living faith.

The Wu Way sees prayer as a much maligned, misunderstood, all-but-forgotten healing tool. The Wu Way says most assuredly that prayer, active faith, and/or spiritual affirmation are just as vital to any whole-istic healing regime as proper nutrition, exercise, and relaxation. And just as body, mind, and spirit are one, all healing must begin in the spirit. As our world continues to de-evolve toward what the Wu Way sees as the end of the unnatural path, personal, spiritual evolution will continue to become not only more essential, but the ultimate key to whole-istic human healing.

---

[17] Francis MacNutt, *The Power to Heal,* (Notre Dame, IN: Ave Maria Press, 1977), p. 53.

Final Thoughts

It is within our power, and moreover, it is our responsibility to become increasingly realized as "whole" human beings, body, mind, and spirit. As it is written in 1 Corinthians 3:9, "We are God's fellow workers." A more perfected self lies within the core of us all. A core that reflects unconditional love, forgiveness, compassion, joy, courage, contentment, and bliss, derived from the soft, internal, unseen resting place of higher spirit. As this core lies dormant in a state of waiting, we must endeavor to increase our awareness of its presence, remove the limitations that have kept us so detached, and finally, affirm and actualize its higher potential in our day-to-day lives. The Wu Way sees prayer, meditation, and the practice of living in the moment as effective means of cultivating our natural, personal, higher spirit emergence. Finally, it is natural and necessary to create a positive spiritual reality with functional power brought to life by acts of faith. Prayer, meditation, and the art of living in the moment activate faith just as faith activates healing.

Jesus clearly knew of what he spoke when he told the healed woman "It is your faith that has healed you." Faith represents something very special–an energy so super and so natural it can only be seen as supernatural. It represents the highest form of detachment, a detachment with the noblest purpose–to let go and let God. Jesus served as the vehicle or the spark to ignite the healing force of surrender and trust within that woman, which then enabled God to do the work, from within and through her. To paraphrase Hebrews 11, What is faith? It is the confident assurance that something we want is going to happen. It is the certainty that what we hope for is waiting for us, even though we cannot see it up ahead. The Wu Way says if you want healing, seek it first in the spirit, see it where it cannot be seen, believe it, find a place to exercise your spirit's highest form of trust, and cultivate it. Somewhere within us lies a soul self or a higher spirit–we must go there in order to make miracles happen.

It is time for the human spirit to come to life. It is time for a more highly evolved spiritual paradigm shift. From the technological to the spiritual, from the lower self to the higher self, from the ego-self to the soul-self, from the unreal to the real. From fear to love. From greed to compassion. From a world dominated by a denser cancerous wantonness to an awakened inner awareness where the ego "I" is surrendered and the soul's boundless love is arising. This is the Wu Way.

8

The Final Chapter

As we look ahead, we see increasing de-evolutionary elements of the human ego making continuous calamitous rumblings, restating the illusory notions that "man and nature are separate," "man and God are separate." Modern man fosters the illusion that he has become greater than these, for man with his new god, technology, is as great as he so chooses. The nature and the "natural way of things" to which man is undeniably affixed appears at last absent from his consciousness, as his compulsively driven ego coerces him further and further away.

Buddhism speaks of this duality as the dilemma facing man which creates the natural tension essential for his higher spiritual evolution. There is an illusory, mundane, day-to-day ego reality with its terminal limitations, as well as a divine reality, which implies universal order and perfection compelling all and everything. Modern man, unlike his ancient forebears, has clearly sided with the first reality, leaving the divine reality and all that it stands for to pass from his awareness. The problem, of course, is that since divine (universal) reality includes man himself, his lack of concern for divine reality ultimately leaves him without concern for himself. Thus we see a clearcut de-evolutionary pattern where man's repeated choices to side with his ego's desires ultimately force him to face side effects and symptoms far worse than he could ever have imagined.

In celebration of his ego, he would create the engine to gratify himself with the miraculous capacity for rapid transit, only to lose his air and water to pollution. In his scientific genius, he would develop food preservatives to cut profit losses; uncaring that he would lose life to save food. Air conditioners would destroy his ozone, affect his immunity, his food sources, and his ageless relationship with his life-giving sun, the center of his solar system. He would create for himself, through extraordinary technology, the medium of television for entertainment and relaxation, only to see it program his psyche with enough aggressive violence, abuse, and sex that his own mind with its natural sense of justice would one day vanish like his air and water. His utter disregard for nature, the natural order, and himself as a member of the Earthly community would ultimately take on systemic implications beyond his wildest dreams.

Ancient man, fully conscious of interconnectedness, knew all too well that he only shared the universe and the Earth, and that cooperation was, therefore, a vital element for his survival. Modern man would one day replace this need to cooperate with a terminal, alienating drive of greed. He would then see all his cherished institutions crumble before him, including those most hallowed–marriage and family. He would see his governments fall, with high officials accused of scandals that founding forebears never could have imagined. Somewhere, long ago, he made the decision to choose the road to the left and disregard the road to the right. His would be a path of ego without soul, man without God, greed without cooperation. His inner sense and sensitivity would disappear.

However, nature will return him to the crossroad and again allow him to make the choice. Only this time, he will know that the path to the left has run out of road. He will catch a frightening glimpse of his last days; he will see before him his last hope and his final choices.

The Wu Way is the road to the right. It tells us that there are natural decision-making resources instinctively within each of us. There are natural decisions we must make in all areas of life, for we must put our bodies, our minds, and our spirits back on a course that coincides with the laws of nature. The Wu Way is one guide that encourages the emanation of the natural human self. It does so by teaching us how to live harmoniously with the silent, unseen laws of nature existing within our bodies/minds/spirits, world, and universe. The Wu Way suggests that all the natural healing power we have ever sought lies within and before us, if only we would stop interfering with it! In the words of Robert Frost, "Something we were withholding made us weak, until we found it was ourselves." The Wu Way reminds us that there is another side to the de-evolutionary spiral where hope springs eternal. Where the elements of nature seek to pull us back, reminding us that man always was, and forever will remain, affixed to nature and its laws. These higher elements, as subtle thought form, reflect "Right Power," the fuel that propels us on the path of the Wu Way. Right Power was aptly described by Marilyn Ferguson in *The Aquarian Conspiracy* as "power used not as a battering ram or to glorify the ego, but in service to life."[1] Buddhists speak of "Right Livelihood" in the same manner, highlighting the reality that each human has the potential through conscience to "do the right thing." We must stop taking shortcuts. We have no more room for impatience, just as we have no more room for greed, selfishness, fear, or apathy. It is time to take the natural path. It is time to awaken to the consciousness of "Right Power," for it is truly where the path to lasting whole-istic healing has always begun.

---

[1] Marilyn Ferguson, *The Aquarian Conspiracy,* (Los Angeles: J.P. Tarcher, 1980), p. 190.

It is through the guidance of this spirit of right livelihood that we must endeavor to change our ways. There are right decisions to be made about what foods we eat and the types of treatment those foods receive. How will we grow our foods? Will we continue to use poisonous insecticides? Will we continue to allow the manufacturing and manipulative advertising/marketing of health-menacing denatured foods? In our haste, will we continue to turn to fatty fast foods for convenience and pleasure in place of life-giving foods?

According to calculations based on U.S. Department of Agriculture surveys, from 1910 to 1976, the per capita consumption of wheat fell 48%, corn 85%, rye 78%, barley 66%, buckwheat 98%, beans and legumes 46%, fresh vegetables 23%, and fresh fruits 33%. Over this same period, beef intake rose 72%, poultry 194%, cheese 322%, canned vegetables 320%, frozen vegetables 1,650%, processed fruit 556%, ice cream 856%, yogurt 300%, corn syrup 761%, and soft drinks 2,638%. Since 1940, when per capita intake of chemical additives and preservatives was first recorded, the amount of artificial food colors added to the diet has climbed 995%.[2]

We are out of harmony with our natural dietary traditions on this planet. Modern man, now so accustomed to animal fats in his diet, has fully accepted the notion that humans evolved as aggressive hunting animals who depended almost exclusively on meat for survival. Recent studies prove differently. Several years ago, the *New York Times* Science Section published a lengthy article on the primitive human diet, suggesting that meat eating by modern affluent societies may be exceeding the biological capacities that evolution has built into the human digestive system.

The new view—coming from findings in such fields as archaeology, anthropology, primatology, and comparative

---

[2] Michio Kushi, *The Cancer Prevention Diet,* (New York: St. Martins Press, 1983), p. 30.

anatomy—instead portrays early humans and their fore-bears more as herbivores than carnivores. According to these studies, the prehistoric table for at least the last million-and-a-half years was probably set with three times more plant than animal food, the reverse of what the average American currently eats.[3]

If "right living" were applied to dietary habits, a more natural Wu Way type of system eating, with better options that include more vegetable proteins, would surely be employed. This system would include regionally provided and seasonally rotated foods, high in fiber, low in fat, moderate in variety and caloric volume, and free from chemical additives.

Morever, the Wu Way is a natural system that encourages a regular program of moderate, uncomplicated exercise. For millions of years humans evolved in a manner that required constant physical exertion. In the past fifty years we've gone from one extreme to the other, from a sedentary to an obsessive-compulsive fitness posture, driven by media influences to strive for "the Look." It is important to apply common sense and sensitivity to your program as the laws of nature remind us that excess is as undesirable as abstinence. While many modern forms of exercise are clearly beneficial to the human body, the Wu Way prefers not to use machines or computers and to avoid obsessive-compulsive exercise behavior. In general, the Wu Way encourages the more natural aerobic forms of exercise that have been with us through the ages—walking, running, swimming, climbing, jumping, rowing, cross-country skiing, skating, dancing, etc. (The topic of Wu Way exercise and fitness will be covered in forthcoming seminars and books)

Important decisions must also be made with regard to the de-evolution of the mind. It is essential that we gain a more complete awareness of ourselves as complete, multifaceted,

---

[3] *New York Times* Science Section, May 15, 1979.

sensitive organisms with extensive emotional capacities and needs far beyond our current superficial, one-dimensional behavior patterns. We have a responsibility to become more aware of the interconnectedness of our mental/emotional selves with our five basic human emotional responses—joy, anger, sadness, fear, and pensiveness—and all that they represent.

We have to take a hard look at many of the decisions we've made in the past, decisions that have profoundly affected our bodies, minds, and spirits. Just how healthy is the modern human mind? How desensitized has it had to become in order to simply cope? With so many of our life systems now crumbling before us, we have learned well the art of denial. The chaotic lives we lead, the stresses of our work and play, our laws, rules, regulations, mores, codes, and habits are all tainted by the crisis of de-evolution. Our decision to place ego/man/technology before soul/God/Nature in the name of progress has at last detonated the de-evolutionary time bomb, placing great strain on emotional and mental health. The Wu Way attempts to help us chart a course toward a more natural mind. This natural mind state is realized as our natural emotional self emerges through confrontation/release, acceptance/forgiveness and healing attainment. This realized natural mind-self is enhanced through visualization, meditation, spiritual perception modification, and prayer/contemplation, which are the primary vehicles the Wu Way espouses.

Ours is a worldly world destroyed by excess left-brain behavior and its resultant emotional right-brain dysfunctionalism. Deep within we must retrace to where we discarded our emotional/spiritual selves and make the effort to reclaim those repressed selves. Dr. Charles Whitfield writes, "Through various ways, including being real, self-reflection, therapy groups, self-help groups, and counseling, many people are transforming their lives to become more free, whole and fulfilling."[4]

---

[4] Dr. Charles Whitfield, *Healing The Child Within,* (Deerfield Beach, FL: Health Communications, Inc., 1987), p. 107.

Dr. Whitfield reminds us that in this transforming work we expose the vulnerable parts of our emotional selves while paradoxically claiming the power inherent through such wholistic integration. The Wu Way sees it as a matter of assuming personal power through increased mental-emotional consciousness. True "beingness" is naturally emergent and can therefore be willfully denied through desensitization. Though we need proper facilitation, such awareness must be allowed to happen.

The modern human mind is currently unbalanced with excess ego and not enough soul. Brain-balanced cognizance is at last being demanded by the very presence of our mental and emotional symptomologies. Leslie Hart, an educational consultant, who described our educational process as "brain-antagonistic," said, "We are obsessed by 'logic', usually meaning . . . tight, step-by-step, ordered, sequential (linear) effort. . . . But the human brain has little use for logic of this kind. It is a computer of incredible power and subtlety, but far more analog than digital. It works not by precision but probability, by great numbers of often rough or even vague approximations."[5] The left brain may organize our thoughts, but it is ultimately the right brain that sees the meaning. And though our world is currently fully committed to robotic, left-brain techno-mindedness, our frail humanness reminds us that deep within there lies an untapped natural mind. The Wu Way provides a path to this whole, natural mind through the spirit and in concert with the body, with the belief that spiritual awareness represents the most important facet to wholistic natural healing.

The spirit represents the battery within the flashlight, the unseen force within that ultimately governs all other levels. Genuine healing must first begin through the spirit. At present, the left-brain consciousness that dominates our world limits

---

[5] Ferguson, *The Aquarian Conspiracy,* p. 296.

our access to matters as etheric as spirit. This is why the Wu Way first demands drastic change in our spiritually disinclined ways. Attention needs to be paid to the presence of spirit in our lives. We must at last become inspired seekers against the forceful tide of our hedonistic culture, turning to the influences of more spiritually imbued, preceding cultures, as they can serve to teach, enhance, and support us in our spiritual growth. Some of these spiritually enhancing cultural resources may include books on parapsychology or mysticism, the Bible, the Tao Te Ching, the Koran, the Bagavad Ghita, etc. By searching, investigating, learning, and intuiting, we will increase our spiritual awareness and defuse the influences of spiritual de-evolution to the extent that we will then be ready to adopt a working system for our continued spiritual affirmation.

The Wu Way sees this as essential to our mere existence. Neither the paganistic hedonism of the technological age nor the vague spirituality of the "New Age" will survive us as we approach the next millennium. Deep within, far beyond intellect, where the innate spiritual understanding of God has always existed, is where we may at last resurrect our personal/ practical relationship with the universal God. It is through this higher consciousness that we will then be able to turn back to a more whole-istic harmonious posture of interconnectedness. We need to see ourselves and each other as personal manifes-tations of universal consciousness, who each reflect the most personal form of God-potential in spite of the overwhelming, continuous distractions of our ever-present egos. This repre-sents the respect and refinement necessary for Mother Earth and all her inhabitants. The healthier we become spiritually and the more refined our conscience, the healthier our planet becomes. This spiritual paradigm shift from technology/man/ ego to Nature/God/higher-self must be made if we are to survive.

Human de-evolution was the result of an ego conspiracy. There is nothing wrong with ego values, but they represent only one side of the picture. The other side awaits human discovery and recognition. To twentieth century humans, this amounts to nothing less than the discovery of a whole new world. This discovery will transform the face of the human experience far more profoundly than any geographical or technological discovery which has preceded it.

Historical human egos know they are unfulfilled. They are looking everywhere for that which they lack. Those of you who remain locked into exclusive identity with them send out little grappling hooks in search of your missing pieces, but you continue to grapple at the wrong things. You grapple externally in the three dimensional world, looking for fulfillment outside yourself. But it is only the spirit of God that can bring fulfillment to an ego, and the spirit of God is experienced, not outside yourself, but within.[6]

The higher spirit of the human self represents the maximum potential of human "beingness," *the* reason we are alive. This is where life and healing begin. With proper cultivation of such higher awareness combined with faith, healing takes on a whole new meaning. As Dr. Steven Locke says, "Belief is potent medicine." Even Mark Twain must have known the power of faith and higher spirit when he said, "God cures and the doctor sends the bill." Healing through faith and higher spiritual awareness is the most important step along the path of the Wu Way.

The Wu Way feels the greatest healing of all is the attainment of higher human spirit that leads to a natural relationship with God. If our planet is to endure, if humanity is to survive, a silent revolution must begin first within each of us. We must be willing to seek the unseen natural order, the Wu Way. In spite of our inherited inclination to divorce ourselves further from all of nature, the Wu Way tells us we must at last divorce ourselves

---

[6] Ken Carey, *Return of the Bird Tribes,* (Kansas City, MO: Uni-sun, 1988), pp.183-184.

from that ill-advised inclination for failure to do so will surely bring on tragic finality. Both Mother Nature and human nature speak through all of us and through the life around us, in whispers or screams, which cannot be denied. At first, when nature is disregarded, it whispers, but soon it will call louder, until finally it will scream. Look around you. Observe closely the planet; its air, the dependents of its air; its water, the inhabitants of its water; its humans, their bodies, minds, and spirits, your body, your mind, your spirit. Do you sense the disharmony? The only way to bring an end to this disharmony is to stop the denial, the disobedience. With your True Spirit initiate compliance with the subtle natural laws of Mother Nature and be rewarded with true wellness—the Wu Way!

National Groups with Regional and Local Affiliates

American Lung Association
1740 Broadway
New York, NY 10019
(212) 315-8700

A voluntary agency concerned with prevention and control of lung disease and aggravating factors, including air pollution. Works with citizens and other groups for effective air pollution control.

Citizen's Clearinghouse for Hazardous Wastes
Box 926
Arlington, VA 22216
(703) 276-7070

Provides assistance to citizens and grassroots groups working to promote responsible hazardous and solid waste management.

Clean Water Action Project
317 Pennsylvania Avenue, S.E.
Washington, DC 20003
(202) 547-1196

National citizen organization working for clean and safe water at an affordable cost, control of toxic chemicals, and the protection of our nation's natural resources.

Environmental Defense Fund
257 Park Avenue South
New York, NY 10010
(212) 505-2100

Lawyers, scientists and economists working to protect and improve environmental quality and public health in the fields of energy and resource conservation, toxic chemicals, water resources, air quality, land use, and wildlife.

Greenpeace, USA
1436 U Street, N.W.
Washington, DC 20009
(202) 462-1177

Employs non-violent direct action to confront environmental abuse. Campaigns address decimation of marine mammal populations, ocean disposal of toxic and radioactive wastes, preservation of Antarctica, acid rain, and nuclear weapons testing.

League of Women Voters
1730 M Street, N.W.
Washington, DC 20036
(202) 429-1965

Non-partisan organizations working to promote political responsibility through informed and active participation of citizens in government. Takes political action on water and air quality, solid and hazardous waste management, land use, and energy.

National Audubon Society
950 Third Avenue
New York, NY 10022
(212) 832-3200

Our stewardship of natural resources includes management of nature sanctuaries, production of educational television specials on conservation issues and scientific research to save endangered species.

National Toxics Campaign

37 Temple Place
4th floor
Boston, MA 02111
(617) 482-1477

National grassroots membership organization that helps communities and citizens fight toxics in their areas. Provides organizing, technical, and legal assistance.

National Wildlife Federation

1400 16th Street, N.W.
Washington, DC 20036-2266
(202) 797-6800

Over 5 million members nationwide. Through education research, supports judicious use of resources for people and wildlife.

Natural Resources Defense Council

40 West 20th Street
New York, NY 10011
(212) 727-2700

Combines legal action, scientific research, and citizen education to protect America's natural resources and improve the quality of the human environment.

The Nature Conservancy

1815 North Lynn Street
Arlington, VA 22209
(703) 841-5300

Private sector leader in protecting and maintaining the best examples of endangered species, natural communities, and ecosystems in the world. Manages over 1,000 nature preserves.

Sierra Club
730 Polk Street
San Francisco, CA 94109
(415) 776-2211

To explore, enjoy, and protect wild places of the earth; to practice and promote the responsible use of the Earth's ecosystems and resources; to educate and enlist humanity to protect and restore the quality of the natural and human environment, and to use all lawful means to carry out these objectives.

U.S. Public Interest Research Group
215 Pennsylvania Avenue, S.E.
Washington, DC 20003
(202) 546-9707

Environmental and consumer advocacy organization representing the public interest in areas of environmental protection, energy policy, and government and corporate reform.

The Wilderness Society
1400 Eye Street, N.W.
Washington, DC 20005
(202) 842-3400

Works to preserve wilderness and wildlife, protect America's forest, parks, rivers, and shorelands and broaden awareness of human relationship with the natural environment.

Work on Waste
Dr. Paul Connett and Ellen Connett
82 Judson Street
Canton, NY 13617
(315) 379-9200

National grassroots citizens' organization working to provide the public with a source of information concerning resource management alternatives to landfilling and mass-burn incineration. Promotes re-use, recycling, composting and waste reduction.

Other National Groups

American Council for an Energy-Efficient Economy (ACEEE)
1001 Connecticut Avenue, N.W.
Suite 535
Washington, DC 20036
(202) 429-8873

Non-profit research group conducting research and development on efficiency technologies. Also promotes efficiency policy.

American Forestry Association
P.O. Box 2000
Washington, DC 20013
(202) 667-3300

Citizens' organization for conservation of trees and forests. Local and national education and action promoting stewardship of national, state, private, and urban forests.

American Rivers
801 Pennsylvania Avenue, S.E.
Suite 303
Washington, DC 20003
(202) 547-6900

National organization dedicated to the preservation of the nation's remaining free-flowing rivers and their landscapes for fishing, boating, hiking, scenery, and wildlife. Measures results in river miles and streamside acres protected.

Americans for the Environment
1400 16th Street, N.W.
Washington, DC 20036
(202) 797-6665

National non-profit, non-partisan educational institution, serves as a political skills training arm for the environmental community.

Bio Integral Resource Center
P.O. Box 8267
Berkeley, CA 94707
(415) 524-2567

Non-profit organization that provides practical information on least toxic pest management methods. You can receive BIRC's catalog of publications by sending $1.

Center for Marine Conservation
1725 DeSales Street, N.W.
Suite 500
Washington, DC 20036
(202) 429-5609

Dedicated to the conservation of endangered and threatened species and their marine habitats, with focus on research, policy analysis, education, and public information and involvement.

Center for Science in the Public Interest
1501 16th Street, N.W.
Washington, DC 20036
(202) 332-9110

Investigates consumer, food and nutrition issues, publishes reports, and initiates legal action.

The Conservation Foundation/World Wildlife Fund
1250 24th Street, N.W.
Washington, DC 20037
(202) 293-4800

Performs research and public education on land use, toxic substances, water resources, environmental dispute resolution, and air pollution control.

The Consumer Pesticide Project
425 Mississippi Street
San Francisco, CA 94131
(415) 826-6314

Provides organizing assistance for citizens to persuade supermarket managers and chains to adopt a pesticide reduction program.

Defenders of Wildlife
1244 19th Street, N.W.
Washington, DC 20036
(202) 659-9510

Protects wild animals and plants, especially endangered species; preserves habitats on land and sea; prevents wildlife deaths from poisons, pollutants, marine entanglement; promotes wildlife education.

Earth Island Institute
300 Broadway
Suite 28
San Francisco, CA 94133
(415) 788-3666

Initiates and supports internationally-oriented action projects for the protection and restoration of the environment.

Energy Conservation Coalition

1525 New Hampshire Avenue, N.W.
Washington, DC 20036
(202) 745-4874

A project of Environmental Action Foundation. Members of the 20-member coalition include national, consumer, environmental, church and scientific organizations. Promotes federal and state efficiency policies.

Environmental Action Foundation

1525 New Hampshire Avenue, N.W.
Washington, DC 20036
(202) 745-4879

Promotes a healthy and sustainable environment focusing on toxic pollutions, energy, solid waste, recycling, and energy conservation. Activities include research, education, grassroots organizing, and legal action.

Environmental Law Institute

1616 P Street, N.W.
Suite 200
Washington, DC 20036
(202) 328-5150

A national environmental law research and education center which provides technical assistance, public information, training, and creative research.

Environmental Policy Institute/Friends of the Earth/ Oceanic Society (EPI/FOE/OS)

218 D Street, S.E.
Washington, DC 20003
(202) 544-2600

Devoted to helping citizens have a voice in shaping the environmental policy which affects all of us—our public health, cost of living, and quality of life.

Global Greenhouse Network
c/o Jeremy Rifkin
1130 17th Street, N.W.
Suite 630
Washington, DC 20036
(202) 466-2823

Informal network of progressive activists in 35 countries. Aims to share information and foster political action.

Global Tomorrow Coalition
1325 G Street, N.W.
Suite 915
Washington, DC 20005-3104
(202) 628-4016

Alliance of organizations and individuals dedicated to fostering broader public understanding in the United States of the long-term significance of interrelated global trends in population, resources, environment, and development.

Human Environment Center
1001 Connecticut Avenue, N.W.
Suite 827
Washington, DC 20036
(202) 331-8387

Provides education, information, and services to encourage common effort by environmental, minority, human resources, and urban groups.

Inform
381 Park Avenue South
Suite 1201
New York, NY 10016
(212) 689-4040

Research and public education to identify and report on practical actions for the conservation and preservation of natural resources.

Institute for Local Self Reliance
2425 18th Street, N.W.
Washington, DC 20009
(202) 232-4108

An educational and research organization that promotes environmentally sound economic development. Provides technical assistance to citizens, government officials, and small businesses.

Izaak Walton League of America
1401 Wilson Boulevard
Level B
Arlington, VA 22209
(703) 528-1818

Promotes means and opportunities for educating the public to conserve, maintain, protect, and restore the soil, forest, water, air, and other natural resources of the United States.

League of Conservation Voters
1150 Connecticut, N.W.
Suite 201
Washington, DC 20036
(202) 785-8683

Non-partisan, national political campaign committee to promote the election of public officials who will work for a healthy environment. Evaluates environmental records of members of congress and presidential candidates.

National Center for Policy Alternatives
2000 Florida Avenue, N.W.
Suite 400
Washington, DC 20009
(202) 387-6030

Provides information on innovative state approaches to solving environmental problems.

National Coalition Against the Misuse of Pesticides
530 7th Street, S.E.
Washington, DC 20003
(202) 543-5450

Assists individuals, organizations, and communities with useful information on pesticides and their alternatives.

National Parks and Conservation Association
1015 31st Street, N.W.
Washington, DC 20007
(202) 944-8530

A national organization dedicated solely to protecting and enhancing our park system. Offers public education and research programs.

Nuclear Information & Resource Service (NIRS)
1424 16th Street, N.W.
Suite 601
Washington, DC 20036
(202) 328-0002

Non-profit, national information center and clearinghouse for individuals and groups concerned about nuclear energy. Provides information, resources, and networking assistance.

Public Citizen/Critical Mass Energy Project

215 Pennsylvania Avenue, S.E.
Washington, DC 20003
(202) 546-4996

Non-profit research and advocacy organization founded to oppose nuclear power and promote safer energy alternatives such as energy efficiency and renewable energy technologies. Serves as a technical and informational clearinghouse.

Public Citizen/Freedom of Information Clearinghouse

P.O. Box 19367
Washington, DC 20036
(202) 785-3704

Provides technical and legal assistance to the public to seek access or information held by government agencies. Litigates cases to protect the public's right of access to such information.

Radioactive Waste Campaign

625 Broadway, Second Floor
New York, NY 10012
(212) 473-7390

An environmental advocacy and public interest organization focusing on radioactive waste issues. Conducts research, information dissemination, and public education activities.

Rainforest Action Network

301 Broadway, Suite A
San Francisco, CA 94133
(415) 398-4404

International organization working to protect the world's tropical rainforests.

Resources for the Future
1616 P Street, N.W.
Washington, DC 20036
(202) 328-5000

Works to advance research and education in the development, conservation, and use of natural resources including the quality of the environment.

Renew America
1400 16th Street, N.W.
Suite 710
Washington, DC 20036
(202) 232-2252

Promotes increased natural resource efficiency, including renewable energy, sustainable agriculture, water conservation, and the recycling of refined materials.

Rocky Mountain Institute
Amory and Hunter Lovins
1739 Snowmass Creek Road
Drawer 248
Old Snowmass, CO 81654
(303) 927-3851

The leading national advocates for energy efficient technologies.

Safe Energy Communication Council (SECC)
1717 Massachusetts Avenue, N.W.
L.L. 215
Washington, DC 20036
(202) 483-8491

A coalition of national environmental, safe energy, and public interest media groups. Produces broadcast and print ads to respond to the nuclear industry and utility campaigns and helps groups develop media skills.

Sea Shepherd Conservation Society
P.O. Box 7000
South Redondo Beach, CA 90277
(213) 373-6979

International marine conservation action organization, directed toward the conservation and protection of marine wildlife.

Sierra Club Legal Defense Fund
2044 Fillmore Street
San Francisco, CA 94115
(415) 567-6100

Wilderness, wildlife, parks, forests–often only legal actions saves them. Toxics, acid rain, pollution–sometimes only litigation stops them. Represents environmental groups nationwide.

Treepeople
12601 Mulholland Drive
Beverly Hills, CA 90210
(213) 273-8733

A non-profit tree-planting organization. Trains citizen foresters and educates people about local and global forest issues.

The Trust for Public Land
116 New Montgomery Street, 4th Floor
San Francisco, CA 94105
(415) 495-4014

Acquires and protects open spaces for people to use and enjoy as urban parks, neighborhood gardens, and recreational wilderness areas.

Union of Concerned Scientists (UCS)
26 Church Street
Cambridge, MA 02238
(617) 547-5552

Serving the American people through programs involving nuclear power safety, energy policy, the greenhouse effect, nuclear arms control, and other impacts of science and technology.

World Resources Institute
1709 New York Avenue, N.W.
Suite 700
Washington, DC 20006
(202) 638-6300

A policy research center created in late 1983 to help governments, international organizations, the private sector, and others to address vital issues concerning environmental integrity, natural resource management, and international security.

World Watch Institute
1776 Massachusetts Avenue, N.W.
Washington, DC 20036
(202) 452-1999

Research organization concerned with identifying and analyzing emerging global problems and trends and bringing them to the attention of opinion leaders and the general public.

Regional Groups

Conservation Law Foundation of New England
3 Joy Street
Boston, MA 02108
(617) 742-2540

Environmental law organization dedicated to the preservation of New England's natural resources. Works on energy conservation and utility regulation, environmental health, groundwater protection, public and private land preservation.

Gulf Coast Tenants Leadership Development Project
Box 56101
New Orleans, LA 70156
(504) 949-4919

Trains local leaders to mobilize their neighbors to demand social justice and better living conditions. Also works on toxic issues.

People Against Hazardous Landfill Sites (PAHLS)
P.O. Box 37
608 Highway 130
Wheeler, IN 46393
(219) 465-7466

A statewide alliance of grassroots organizations working on various pollution problems. Serves as a national and international clearinghouse for information on a range of pollution issues.

Silicon Valley Toxics Coalition

760 North 1st Street
2nd Floor
San Jose, CA 95112
(408) 287-6707

Focuses, although not exclusively, on toxic contamination in high-tech industries. Ground water clean-up and pollution and accident prevention.

Southwest Research and Information Center

P.O. Box 4524
Albuquerque, NM 87106
(505) 262-1862

A multi-racial, multi-issue grassroots membership community organization fighting for basic rights to land and resources, growth and preservation of diverse cultures and self-determination. Sees safe environment as a fundamental human right.

Toxics Coordinating Project

942 Market Street, #502
San Francisco, CA 94102
(415) 781-2745

A statewide coalition of organizations and activists working to protect California's health, environment, and economy from toxic chemicals.